CATS ARE BETTER THAN KIDS

By the same author:

Cats are Better than Men
Cats are Smarter than Men, Too!
The Cat's Guide to Love

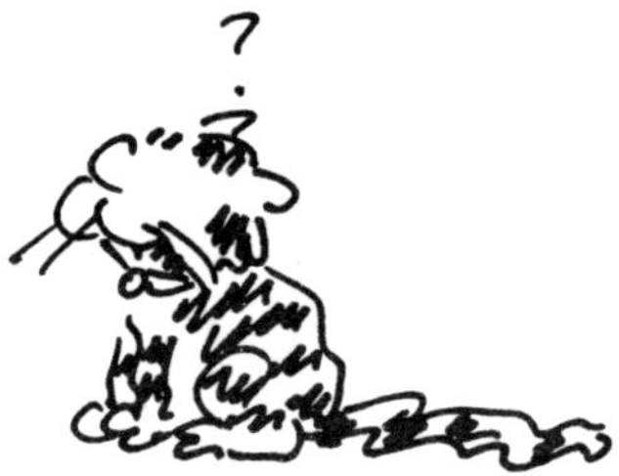
?

CATS ARE BETTER THAN KIDS

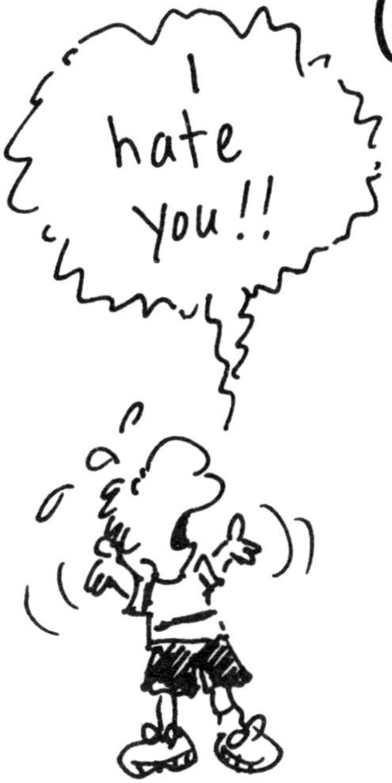
I hate you!!

BEVERLY GUHL

Hodder & Stoughton

Copyright © 1997 Beverly Guhl

First published in Great Britain in 1997
by Hodder & Stoughton
A division of Hodder Headline PLC

The right of Beverly Guhl to be identified as the Author of the Work has been asserted by her in accordance with
the Copyright, Designs and Patents Act 1988.

10 9 8 7 6 5 4 3 2 1

A CIP catalogue record for this title is available from the British Library

ISBN 0-340-68183-7

Printed and bound in Great Britain by
Mackays of Chatham PLC, Chatham, Kent

Hodder and Stoughton
A division of Hodder Headline PLC
338 Euston Road
London NW1 3BH

For Jon and Asa ...

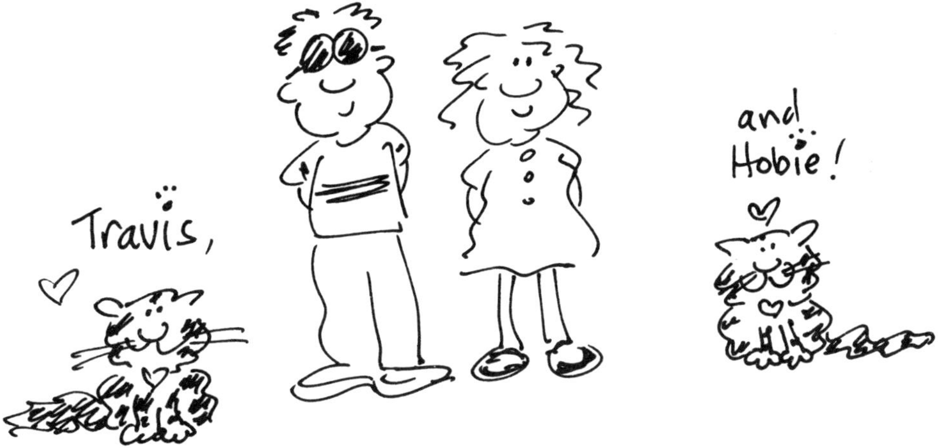
Travis,
and Hobie!

About the Author

Beverly Guhl has designed and marketed everything from greeting cards to mugs. The proud mother of two grown kids, Beverly now lives in Texas with her cat. She is the author of *Cats are Better than Men, Cats are Smarter than Men, Too!* and *The Cat's Guide to Love* — all available from Hodder & Stoughton.

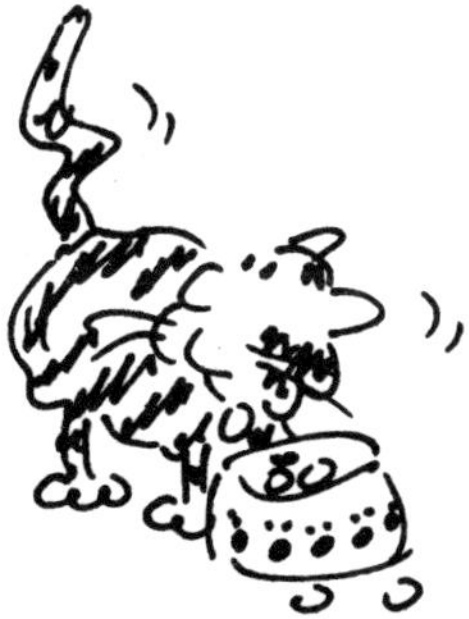

CATS ARE BETTER THAN KIDS

You don't have to fuss
with nappies or potty
training with a cat.

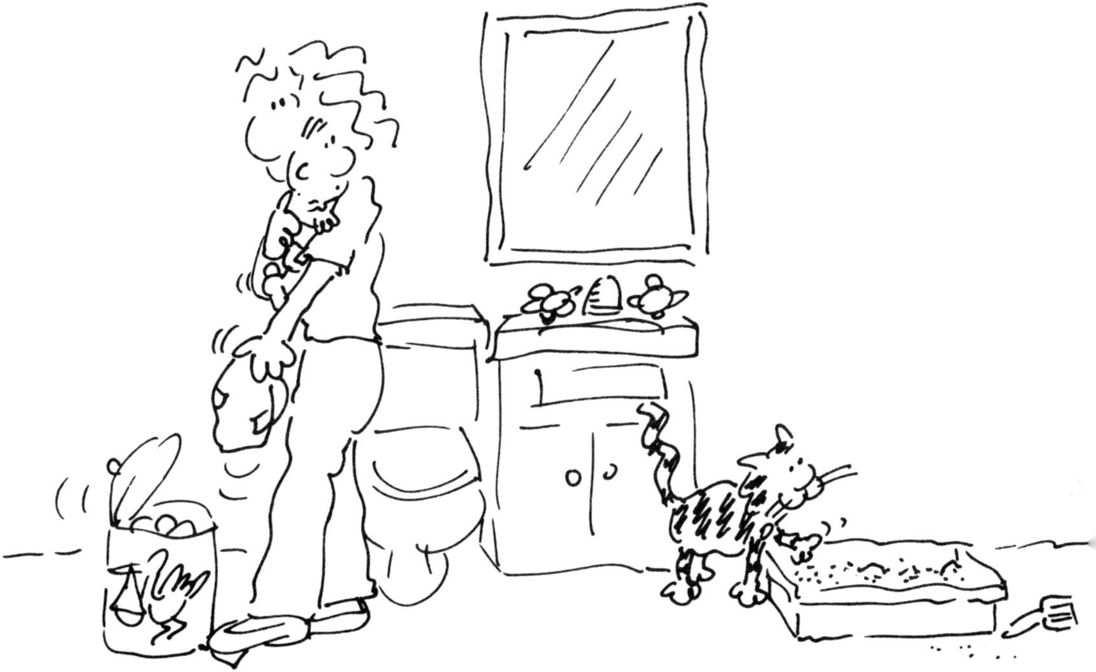

You never have trouble
feeding a cat.

You don't have to pay for babysitters or day care for a cat.

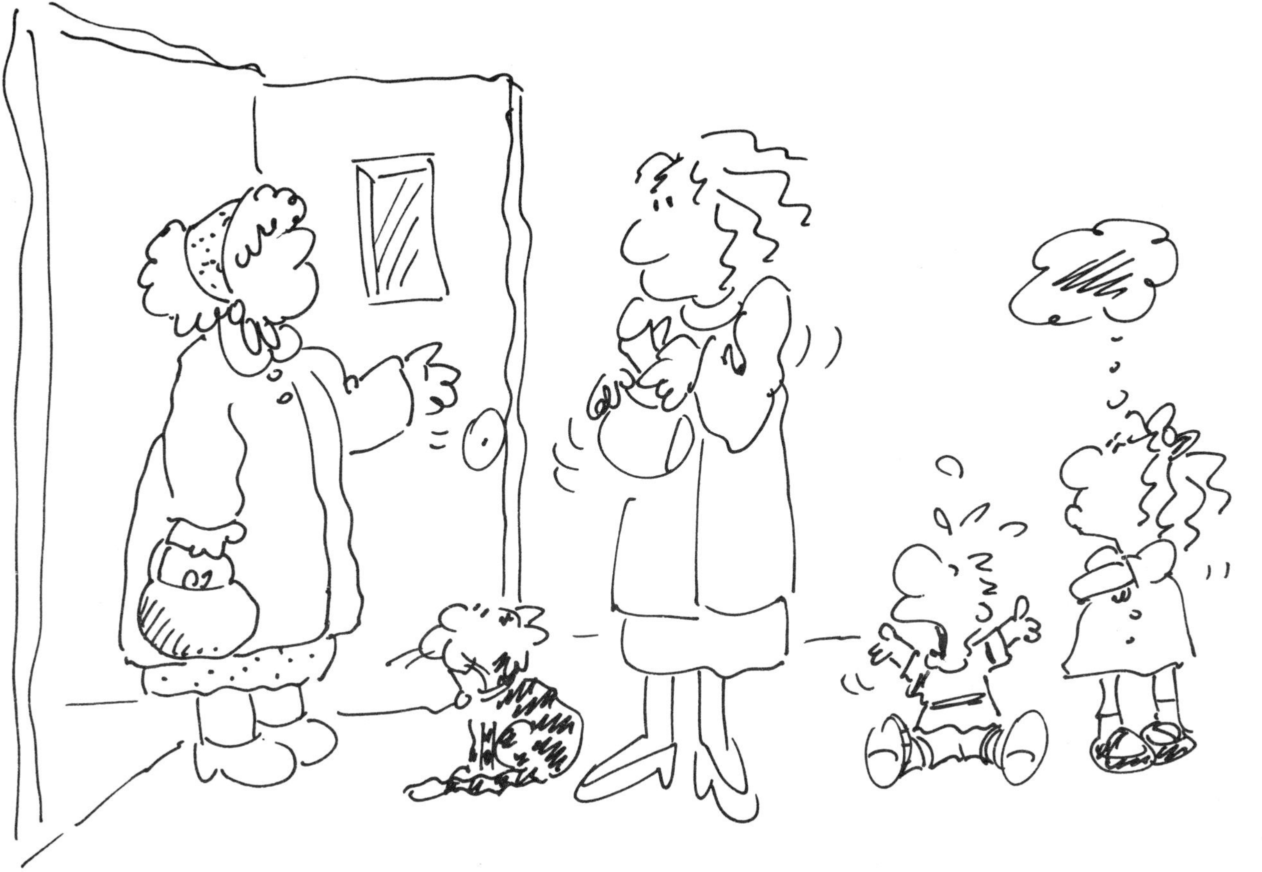

Cats don't wake you up
for 2a.m. feedings.

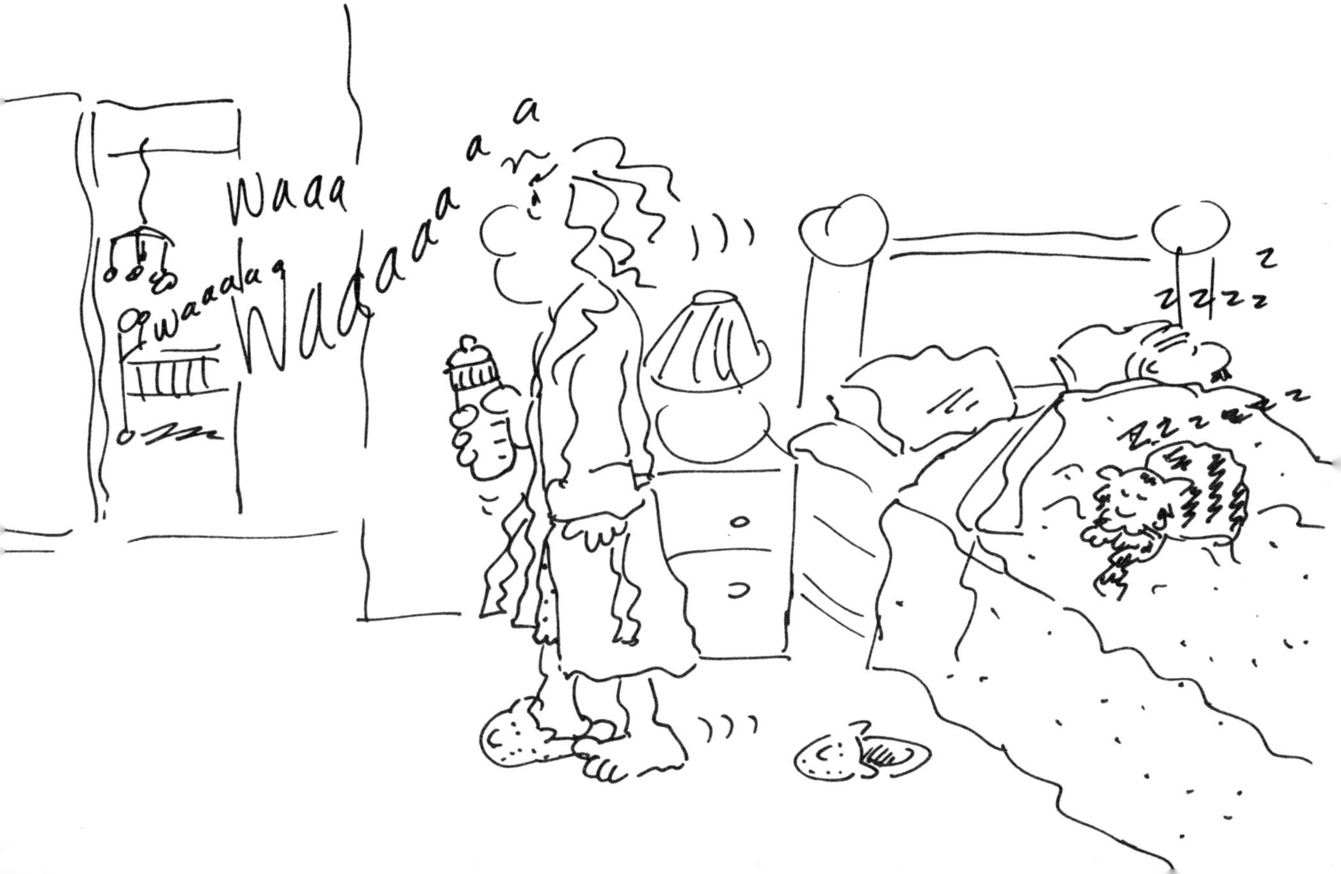

Waaa
Waaaaaaaaa
waaaaaa
zzzzz

you never have to fight
with a cat about what
they wear.

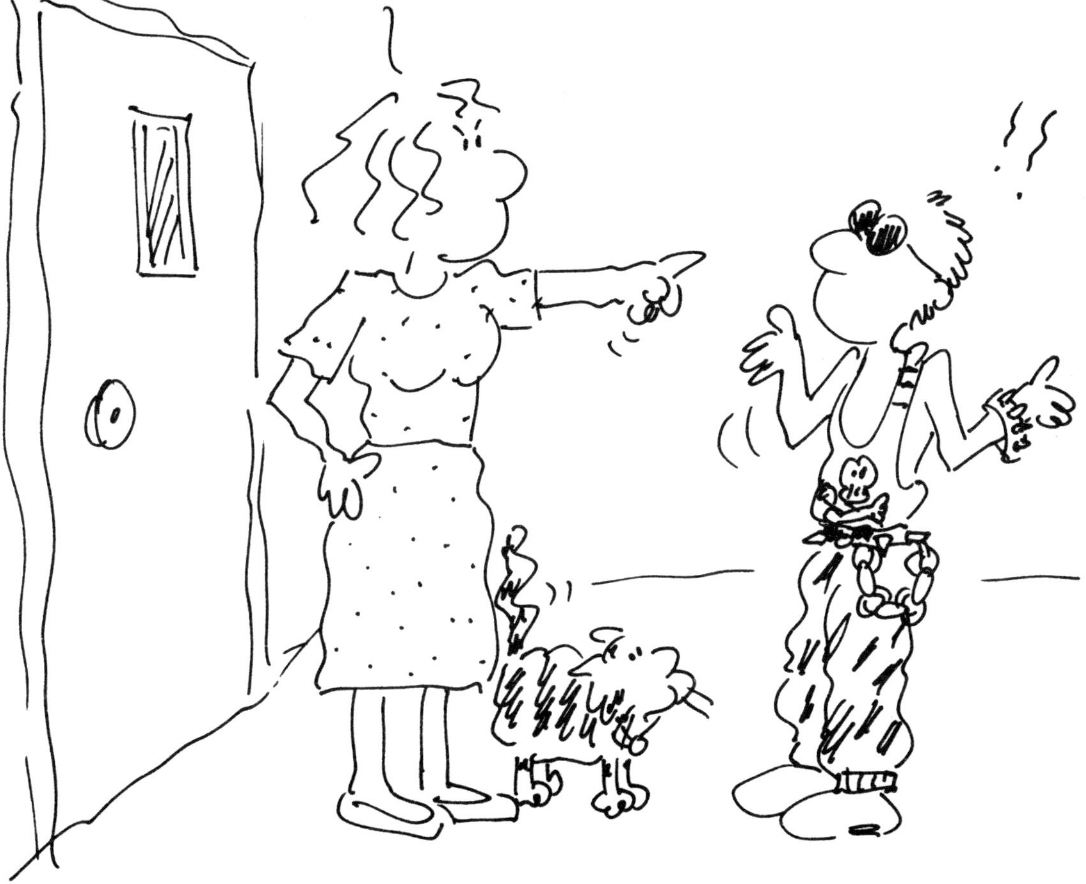

Cats don't ask questions.

why is the sky blue?
What do worms eat?
What does 'tampon' mean?
Where do babies come from?
Why?
what is sex?
How?

Cats never compare
you with others.

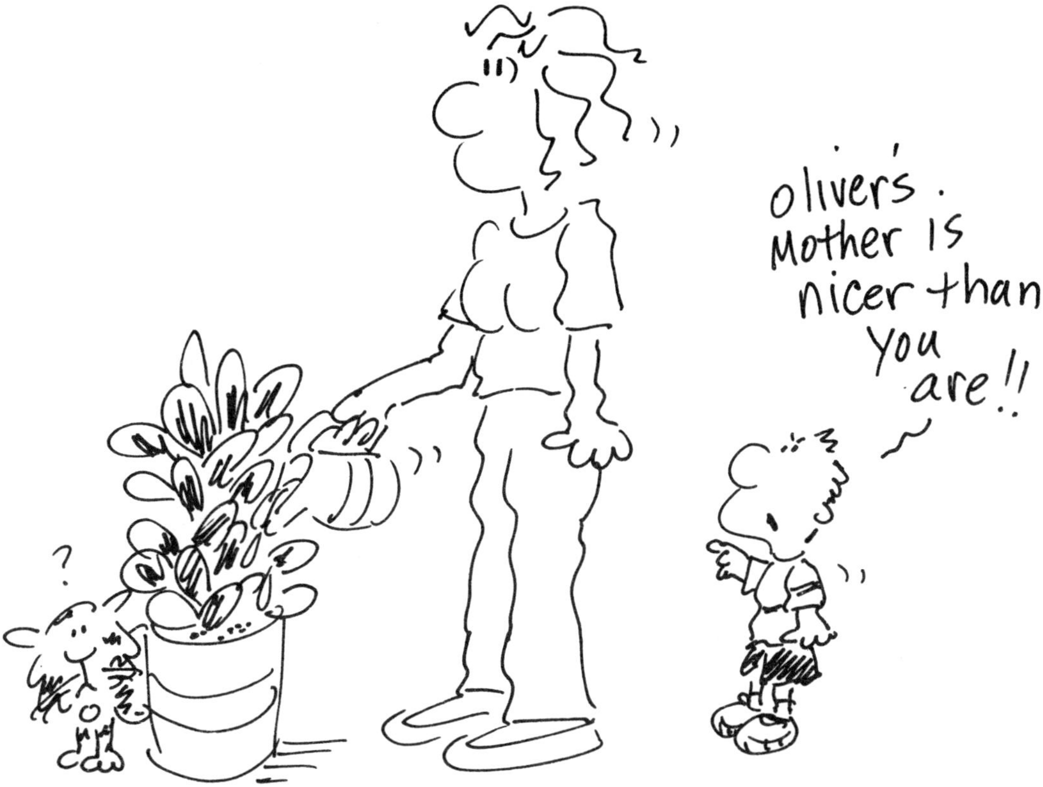
olivers Mother is nicer than you are!!

Cats don't require expensive furniture, car seats, or toys.

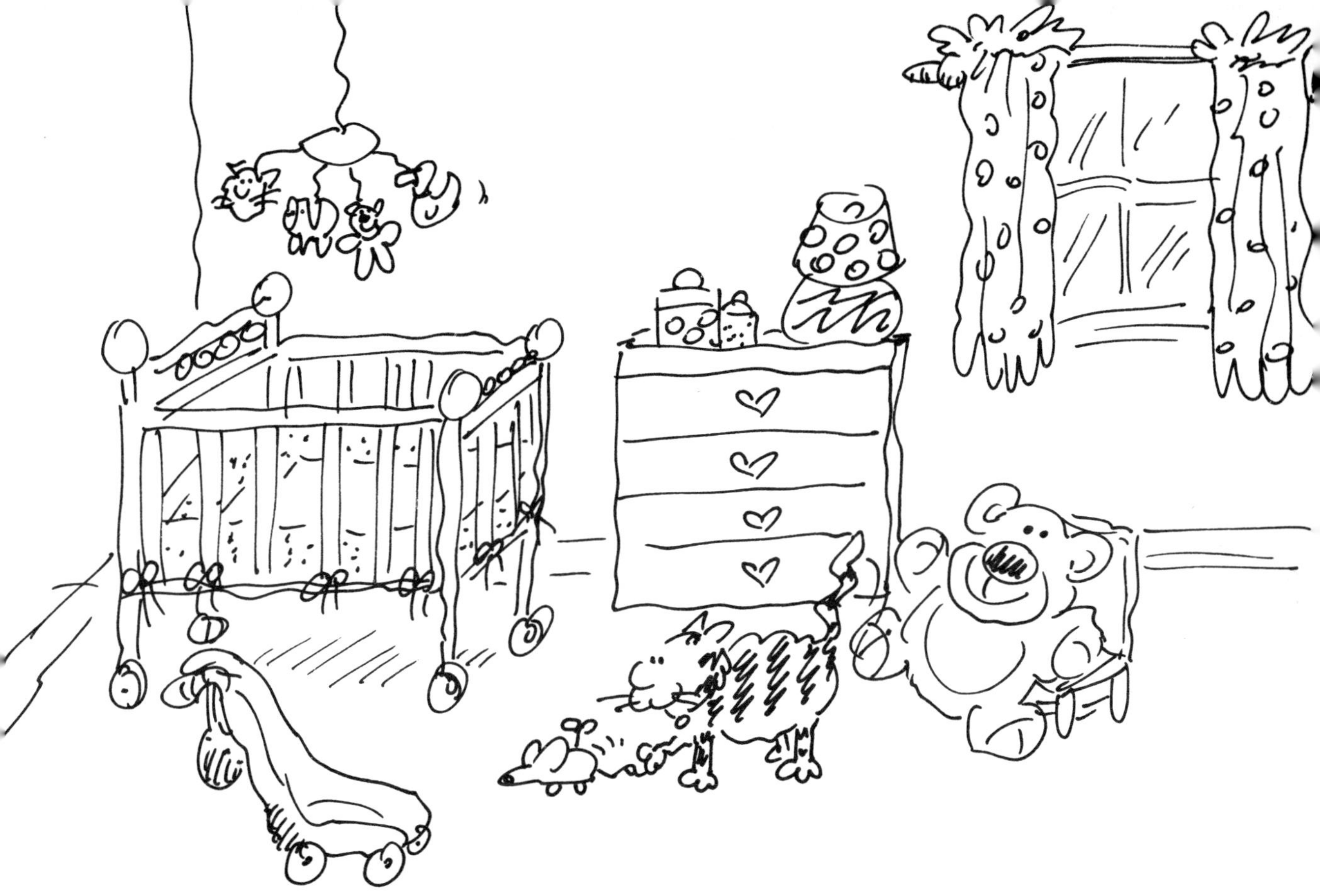

Cats never talk back
to you.

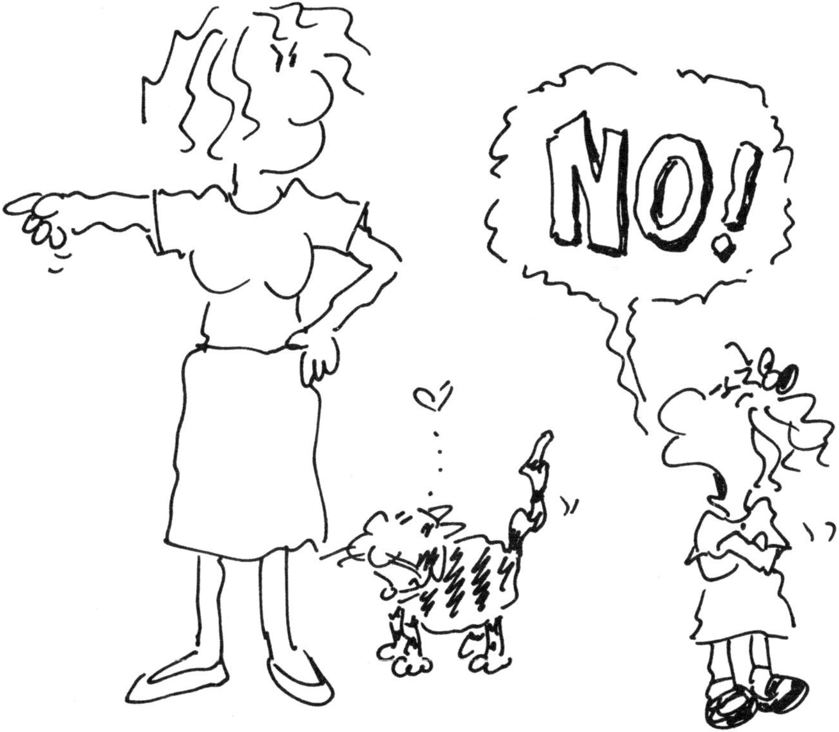
NO!

Cats never break things
while playing with
their toys.

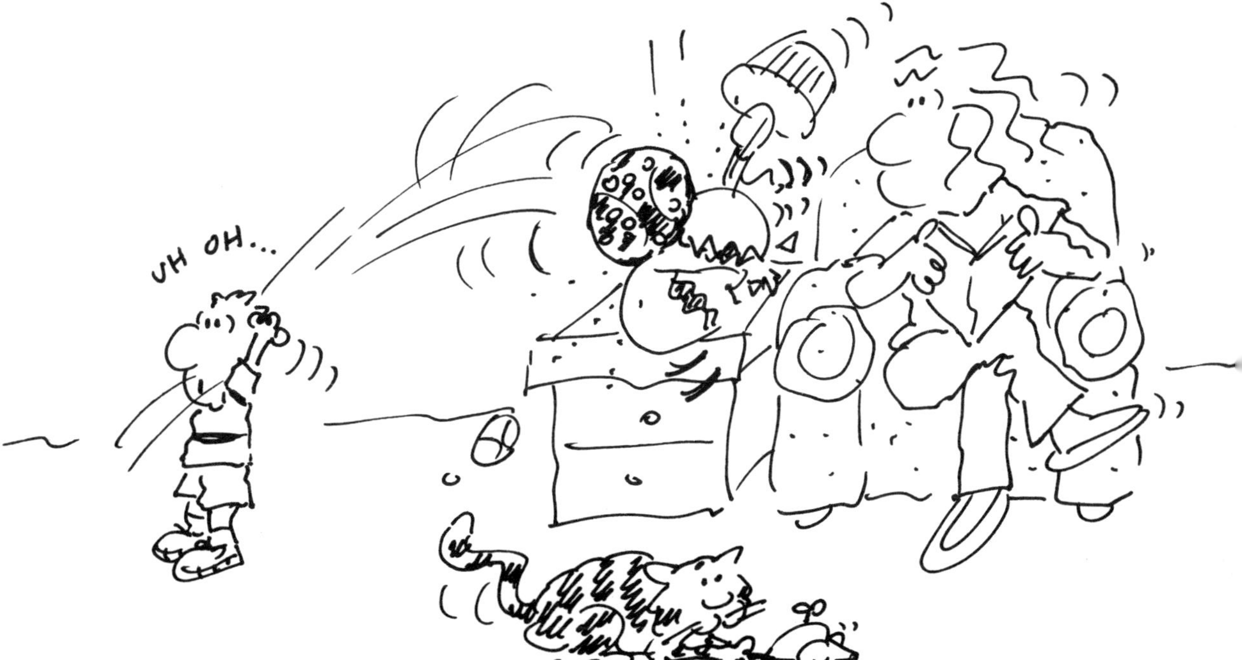
UH OH...

Cats never want to
borrow the car.

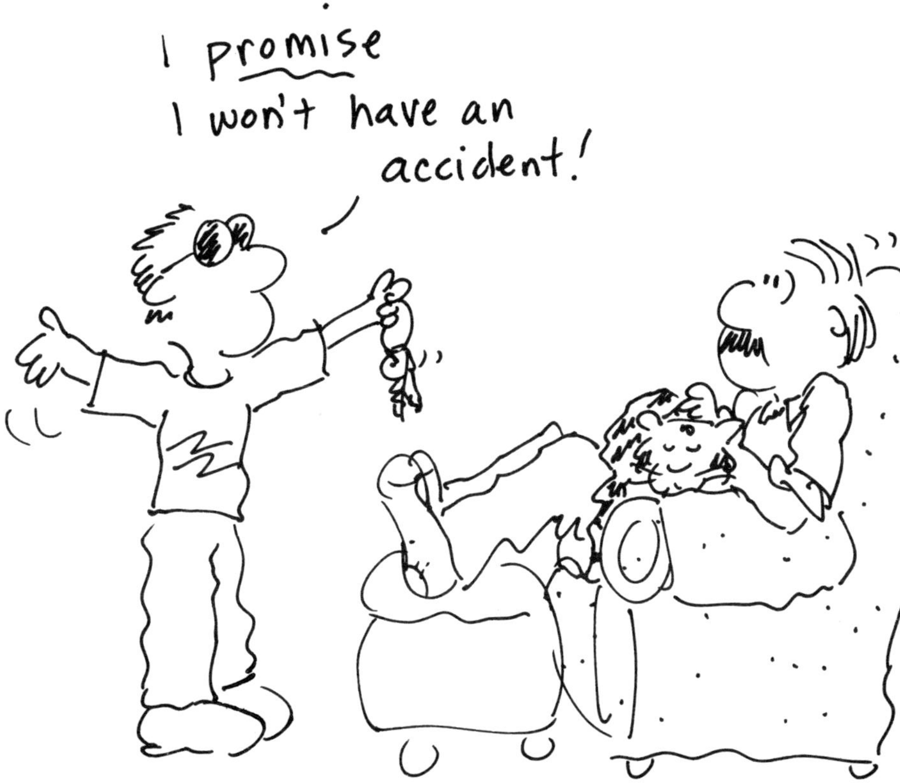
I promise
I won't have an
accident!

Cats never want to go
outside to play in the rain.

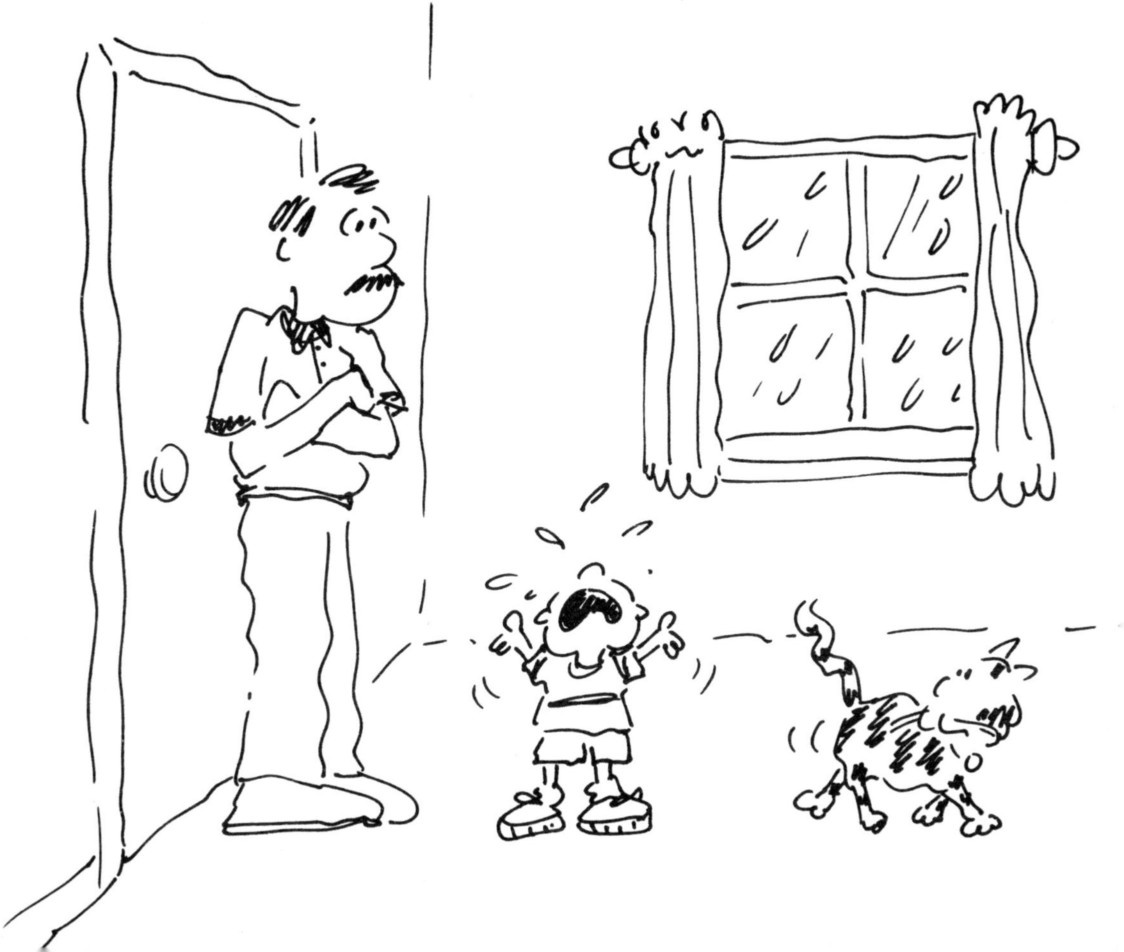

Cats don't have temper tantrums.

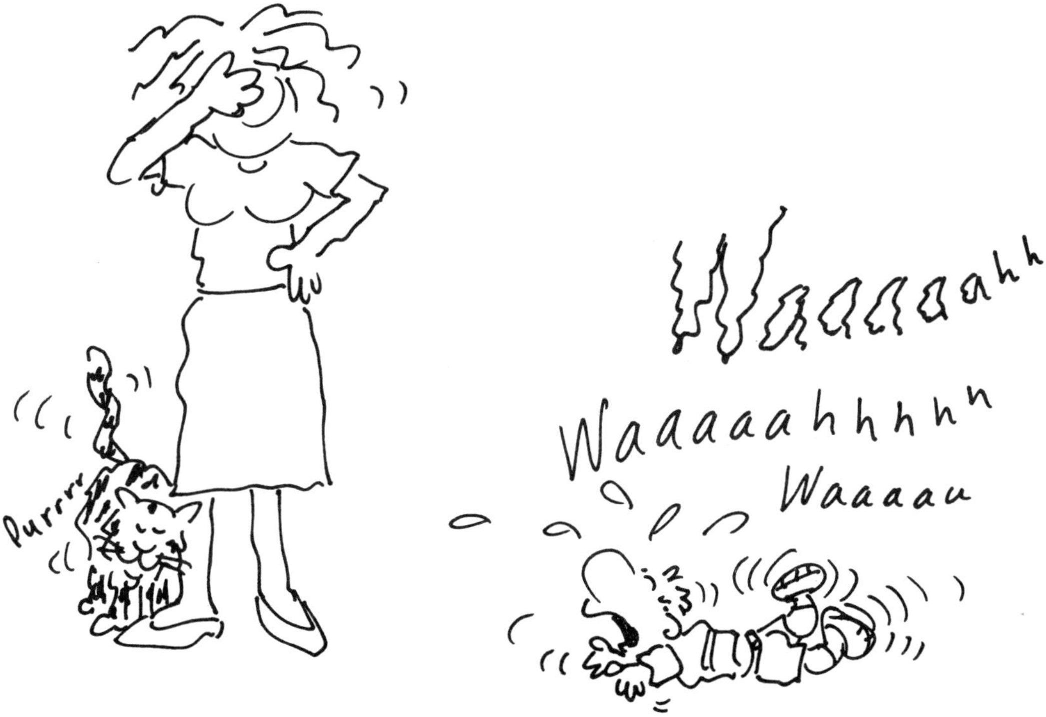
Purrrrr
Waaaaaahh
Waaaaaahhhhhn
Waaaaau

You never have to ask a
cat to take a bath.

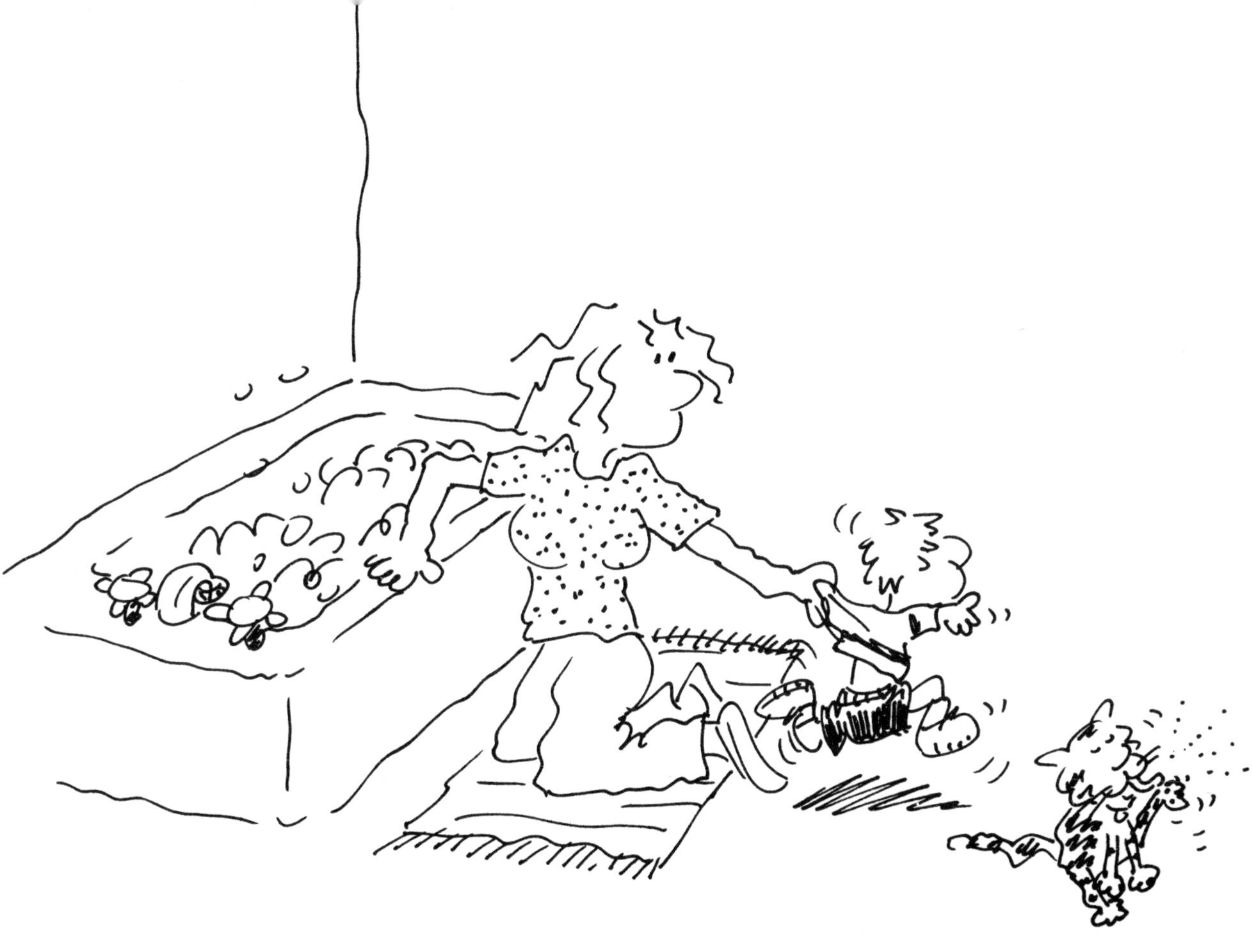

You never have to ask
a cat to turn the
volume down!

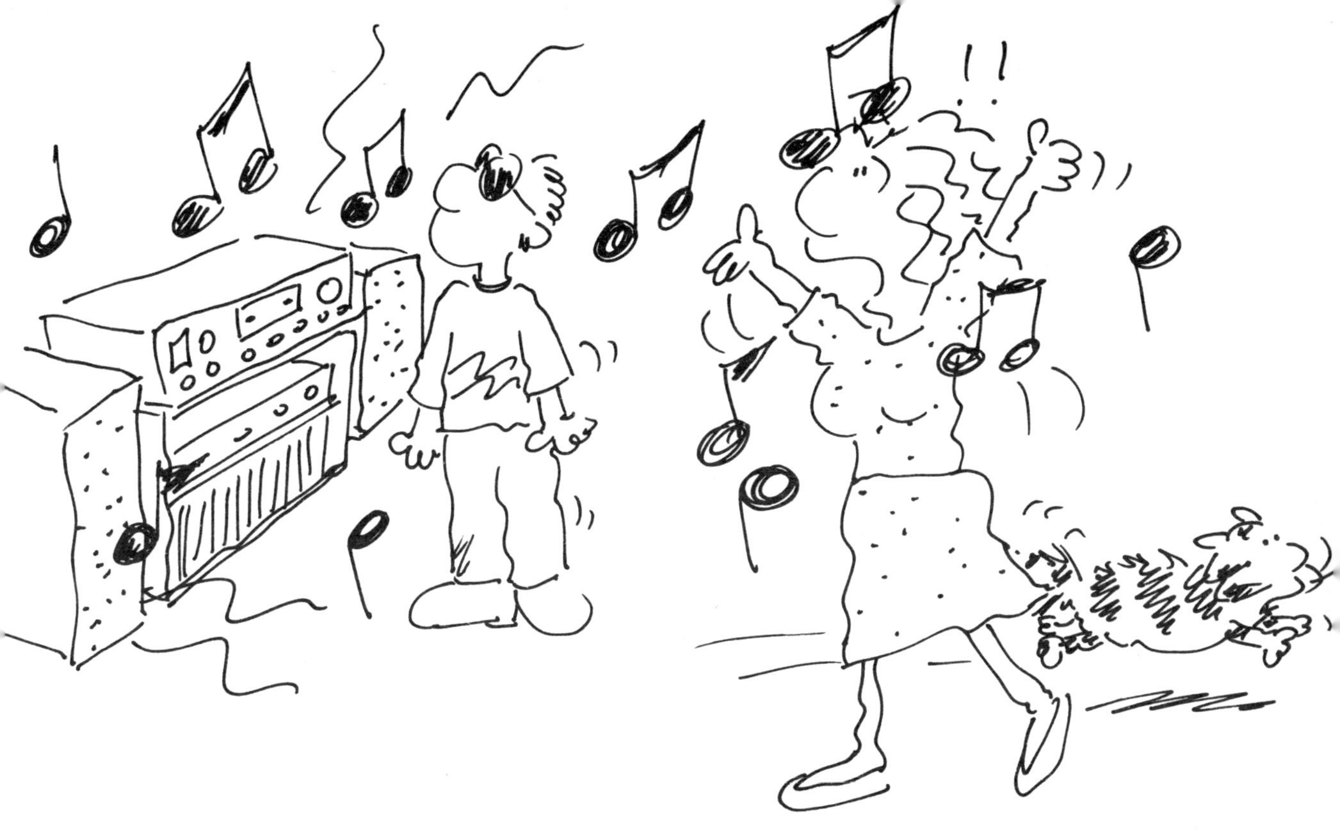

Cats never claim to be
smarter than you.

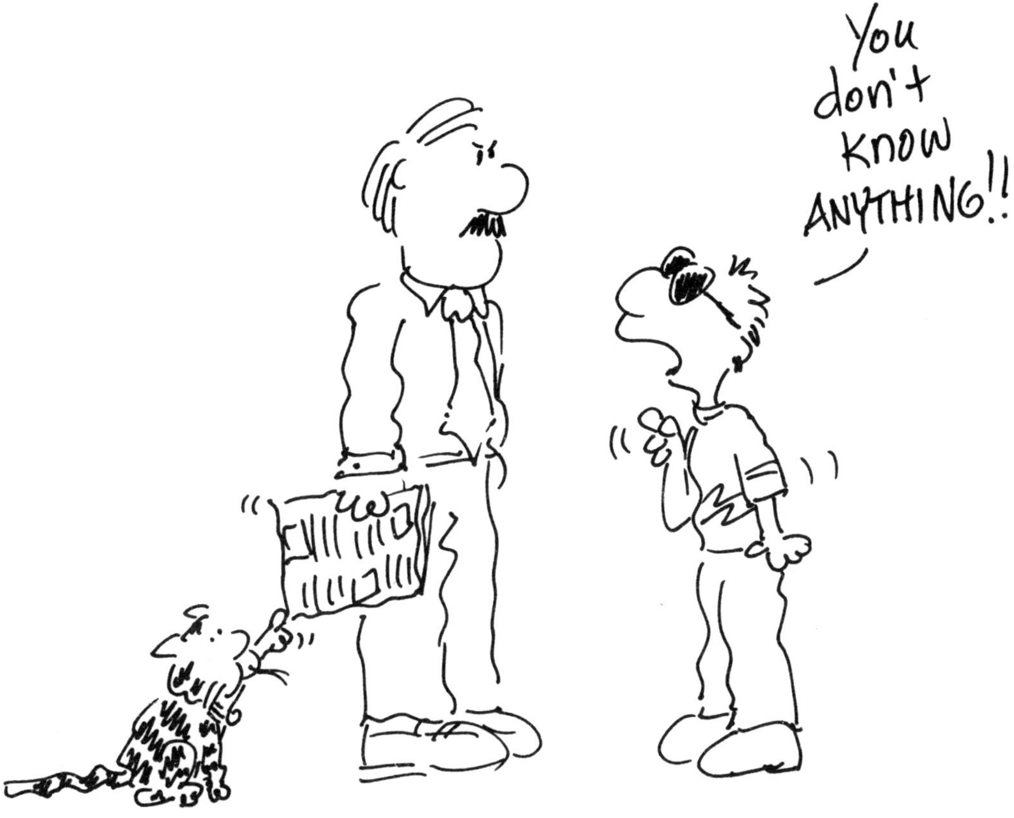
You don't know ANYTHING!!

It doesn't cost very
much to feed
a cat.

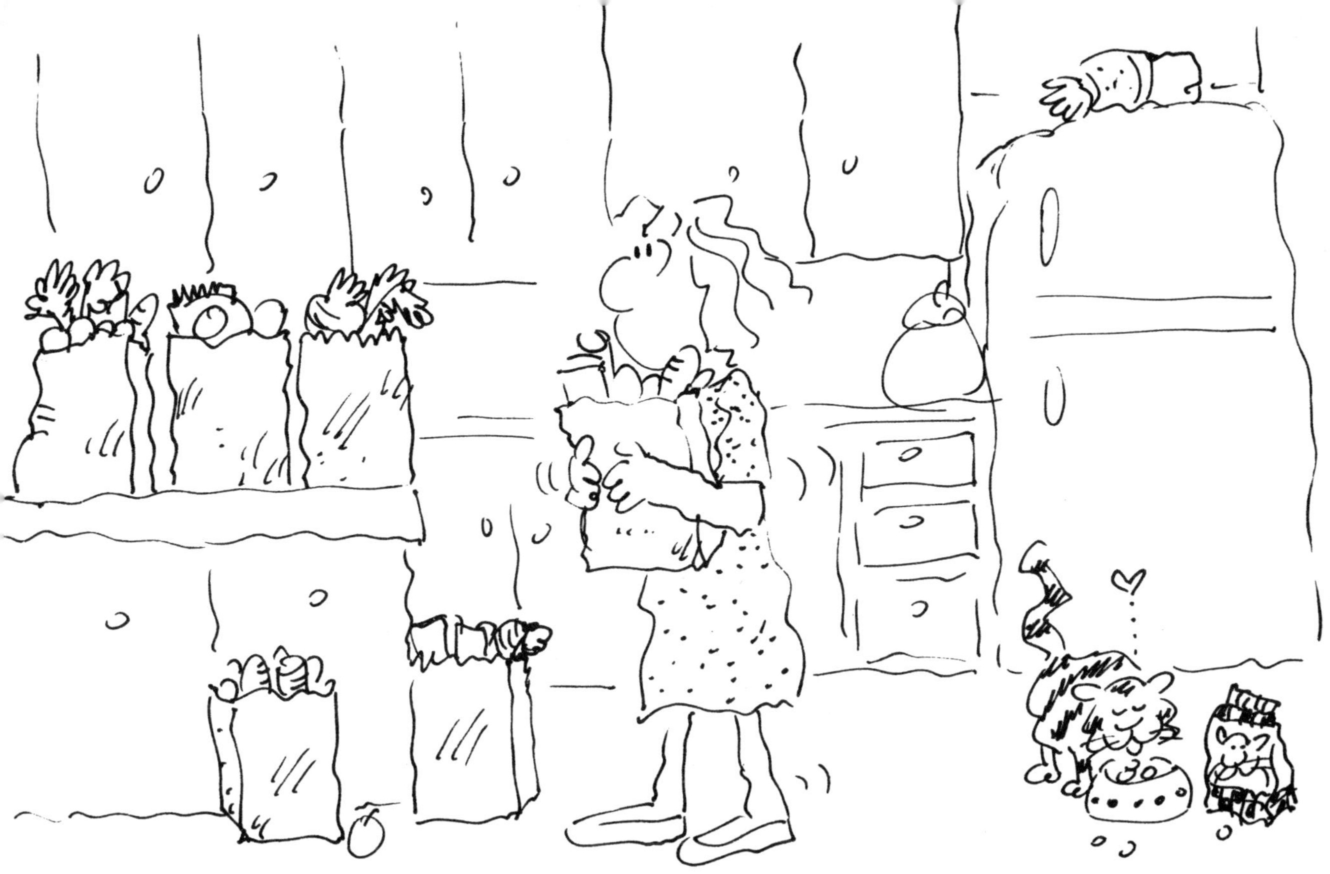

Cats never borrow your clothes.

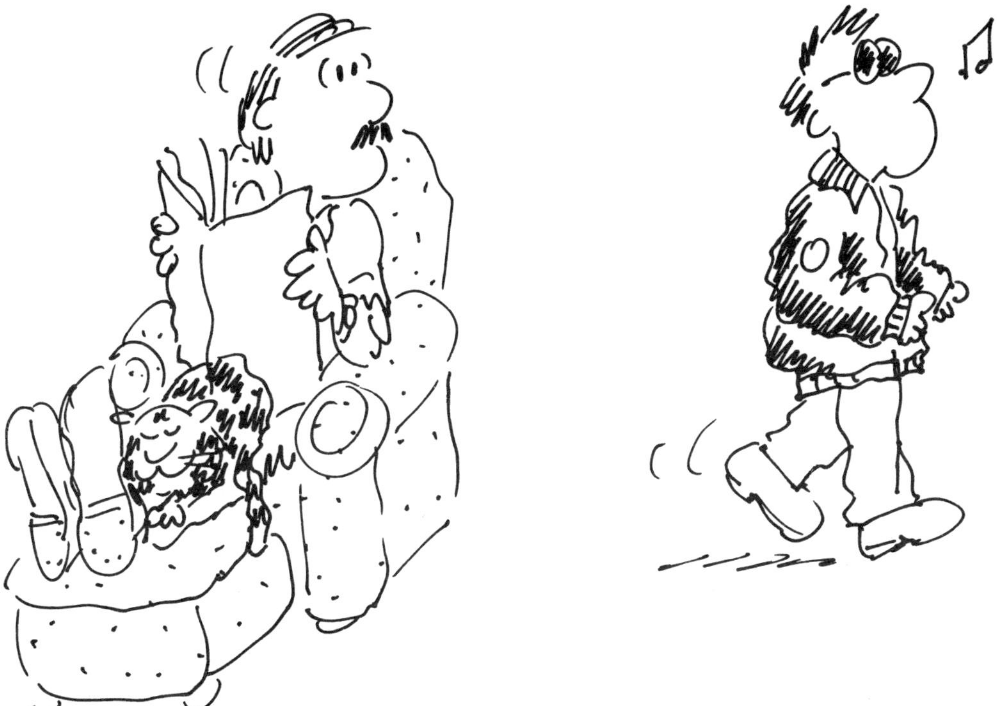

Cats don't leave clothes, toys, and food all over the house.

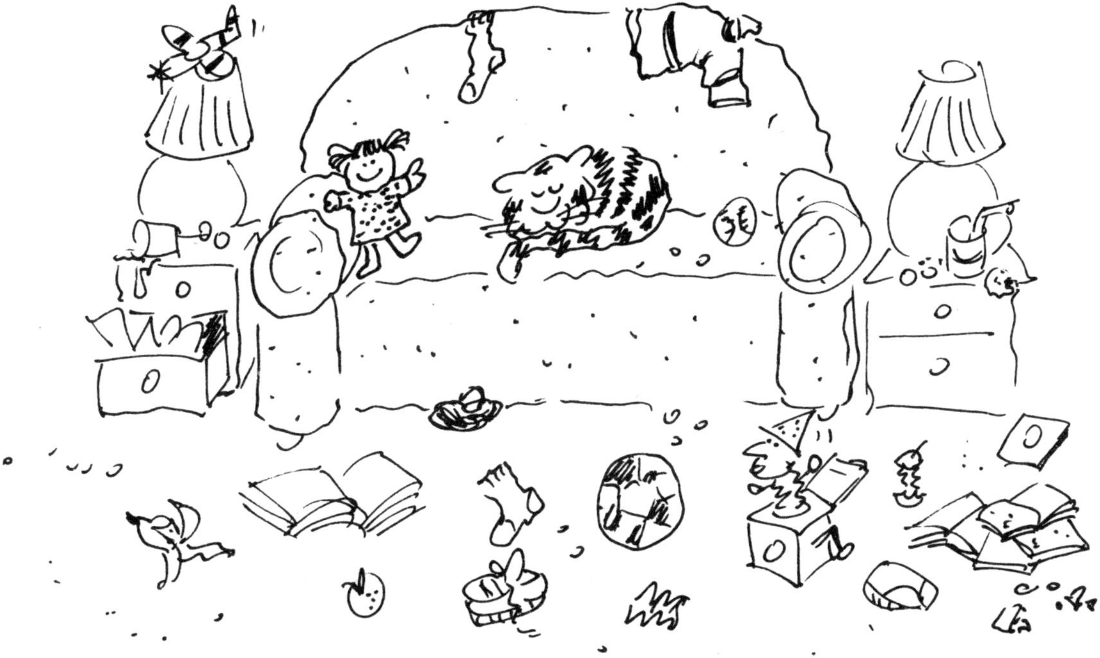

You'd never get a call to bail a cat out of jail.

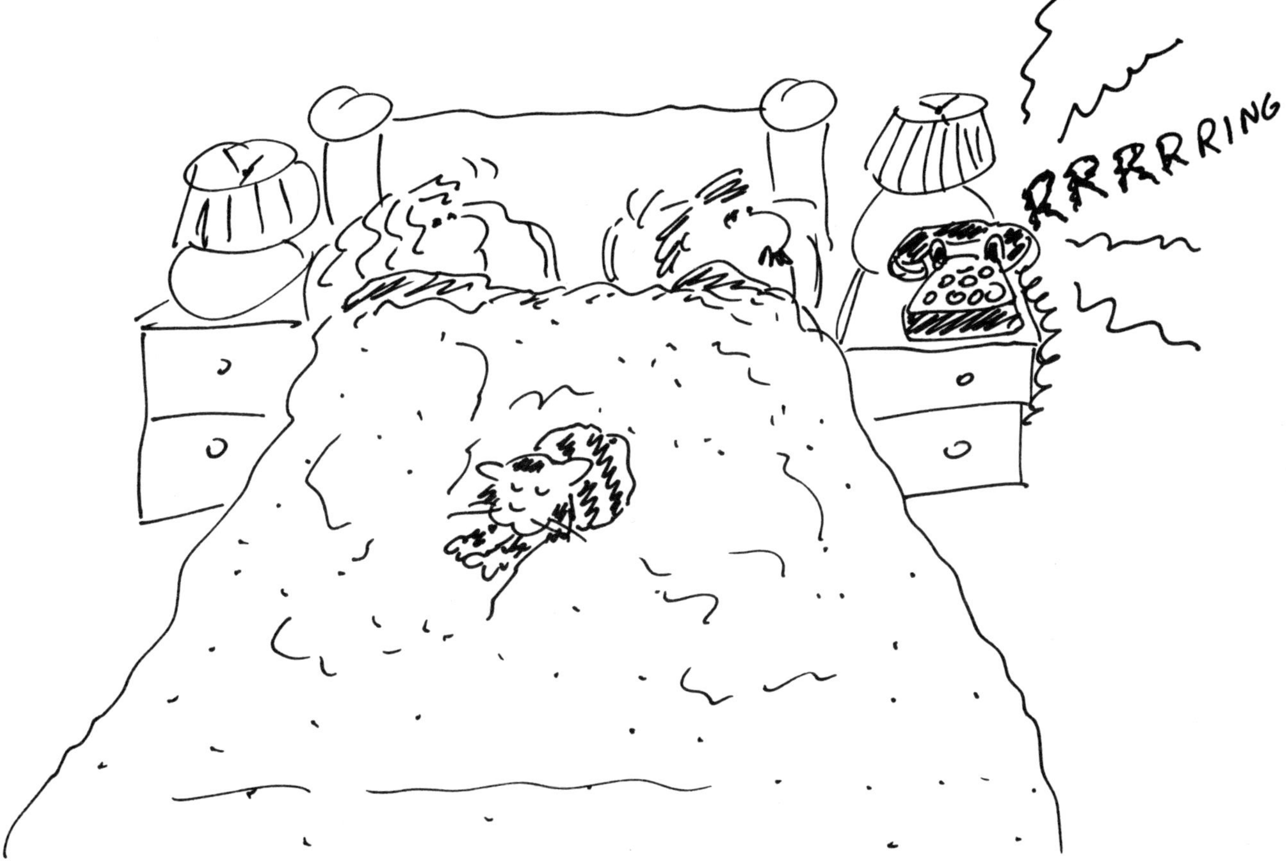
RRRRRING

You never have to worry
about how much T.V.
a cat is watching.

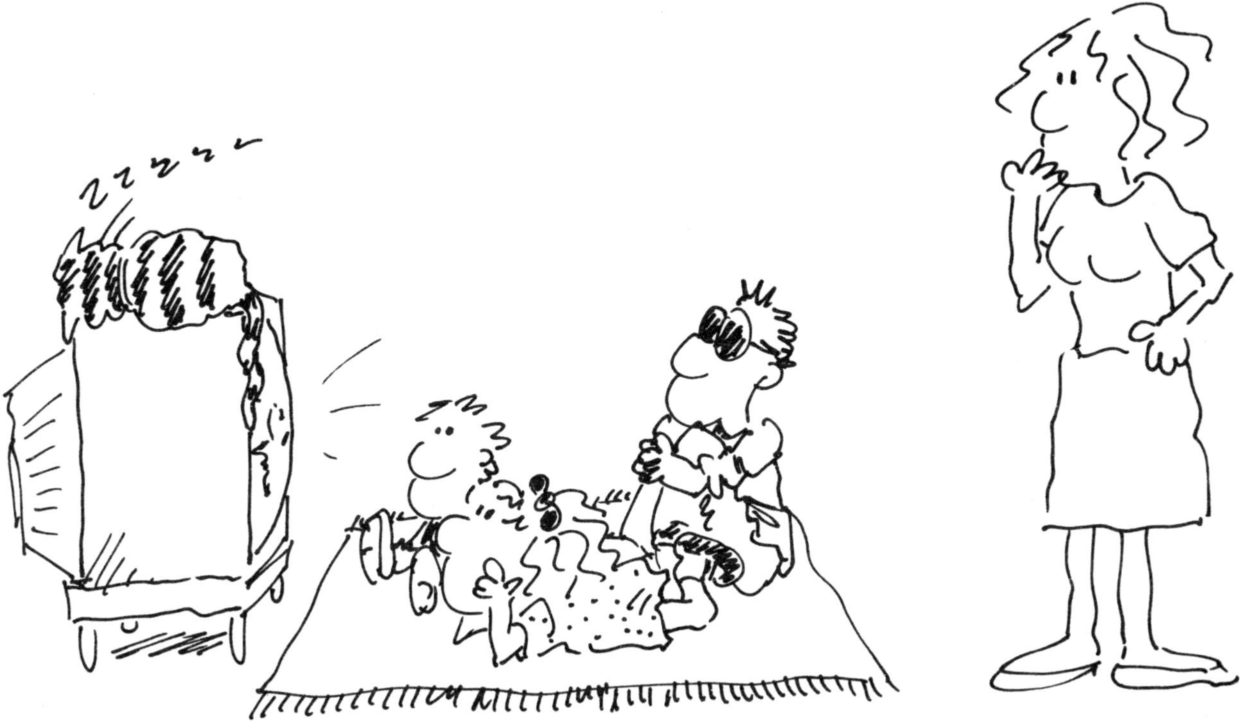

You never feel like sending a
cat to live with the grandparents.

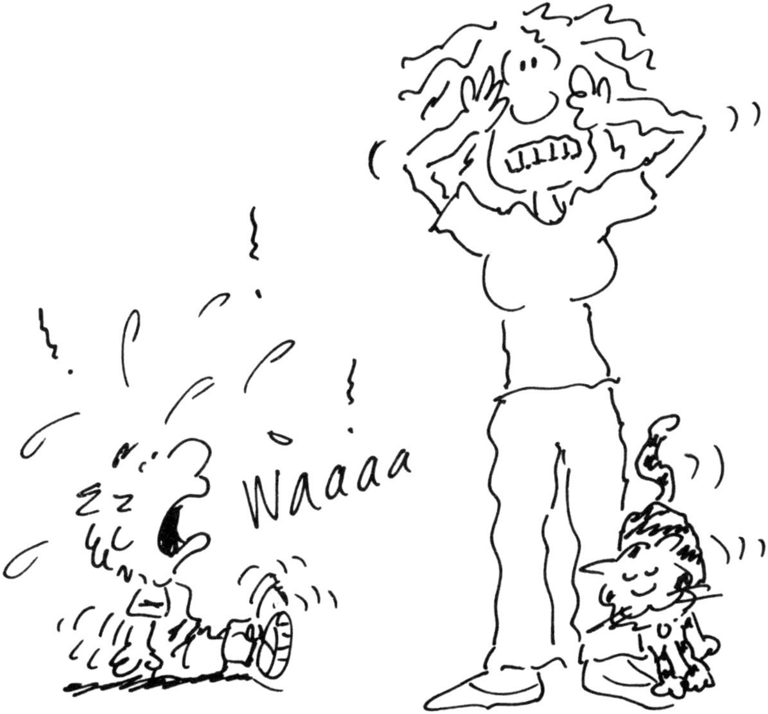
Waaaa

Cats never need new shoes
(which they'll outgrow in weeks).

Curfews are never an
issue with a cat.

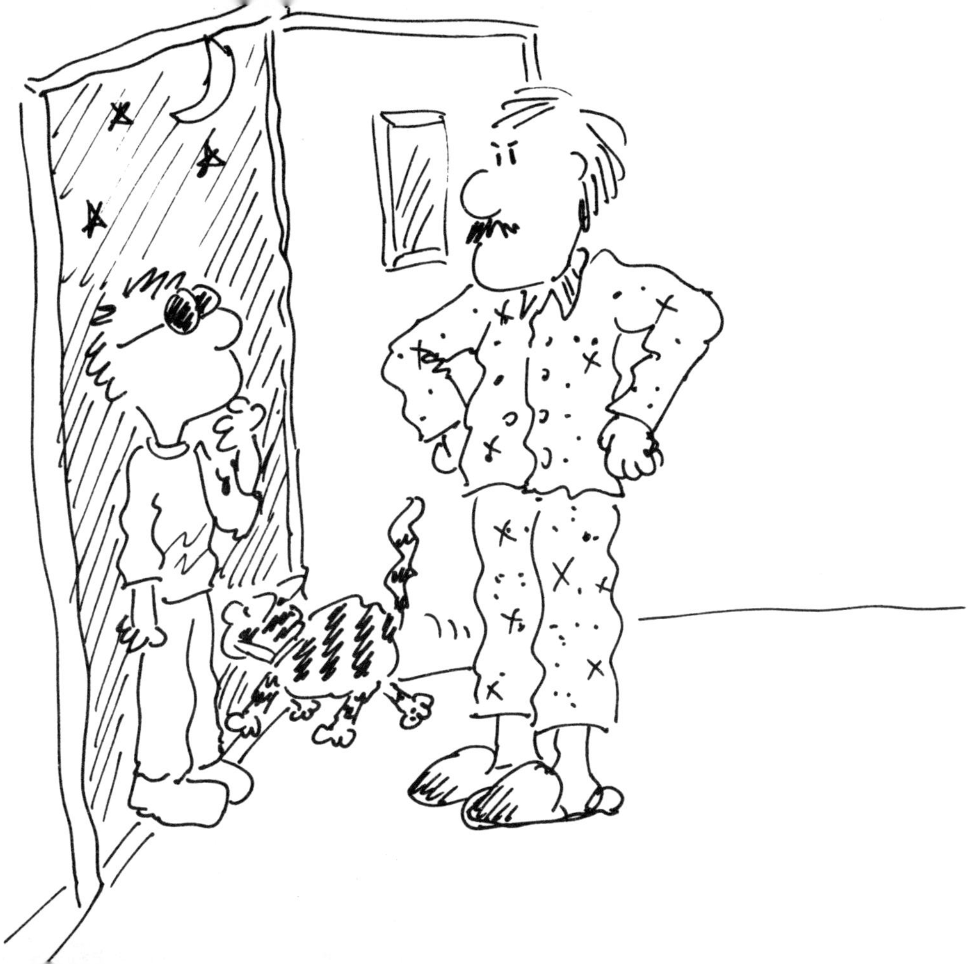

Cats don't fight over whose
turn it is to use the bathroom...
or the phone... or the T.V. ...
or the...

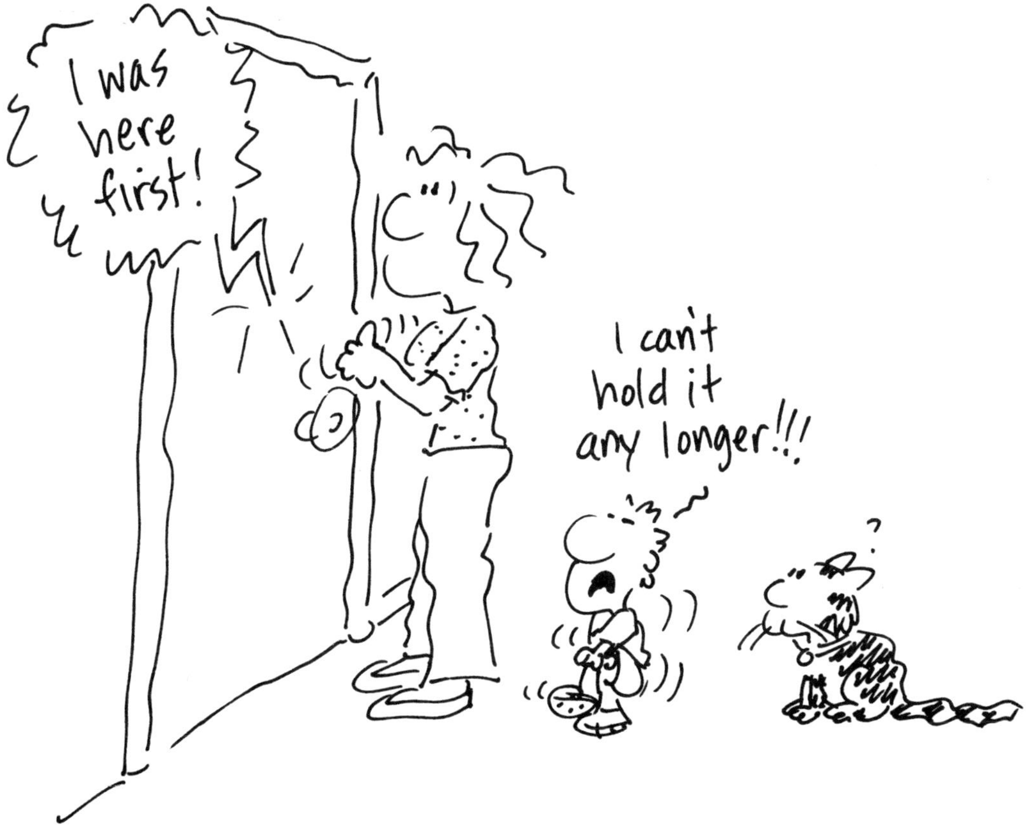
I was here first!
I can't hold it any longer!!!

Cats never want their own
car or telephone.

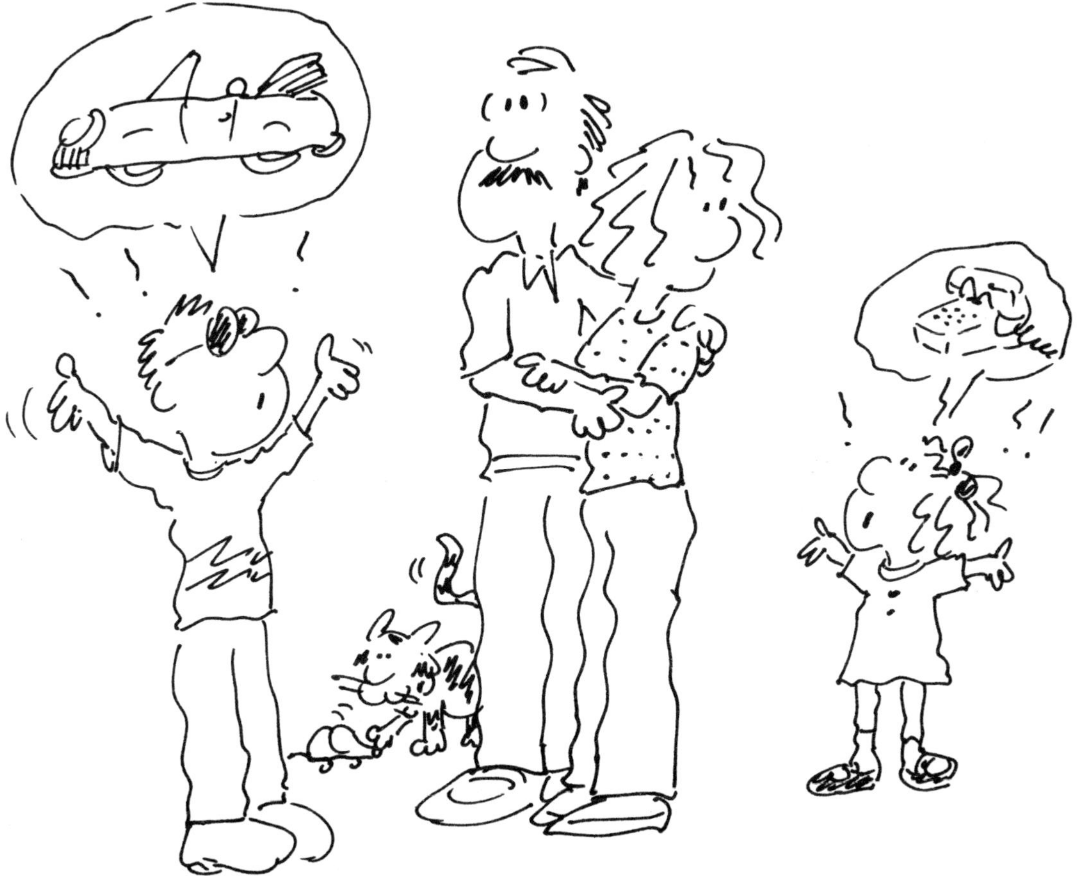

Cats aren't hard to please.

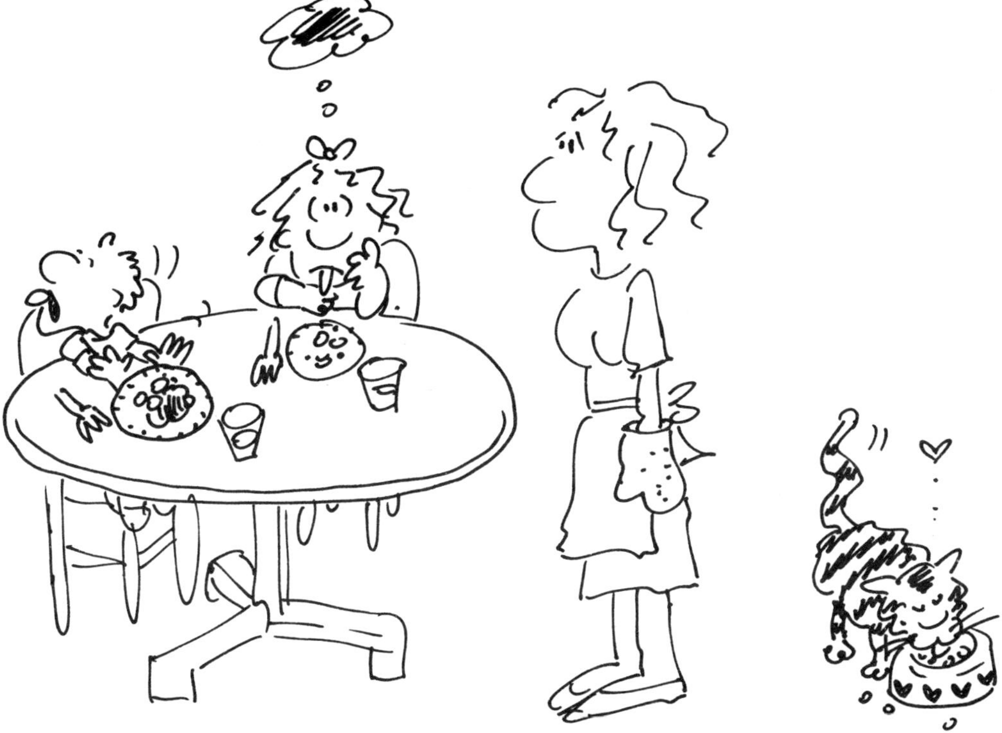

Cats never spill things.

Cats never think you're
mean or horrible.

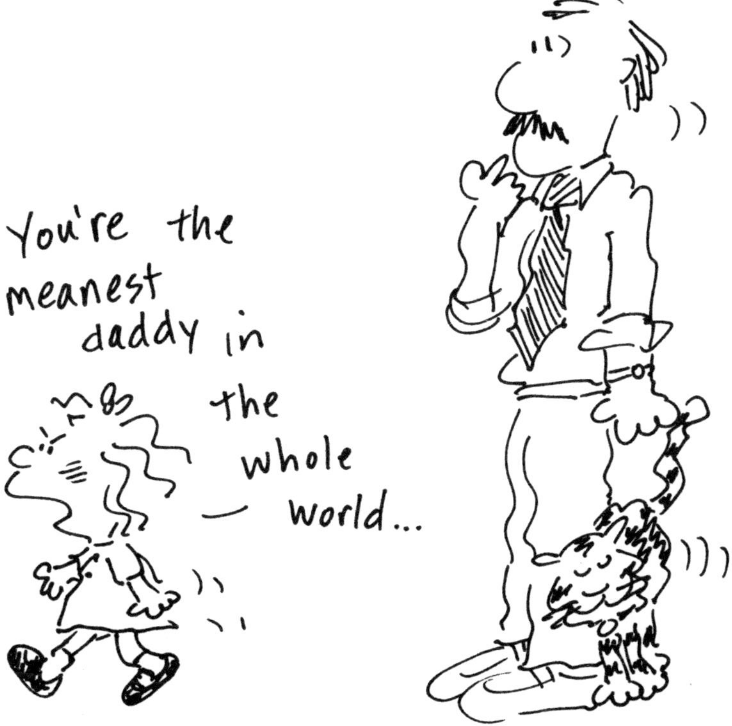
You're the meanest daddy in the whole world...

A cat would never
play with your makeup.

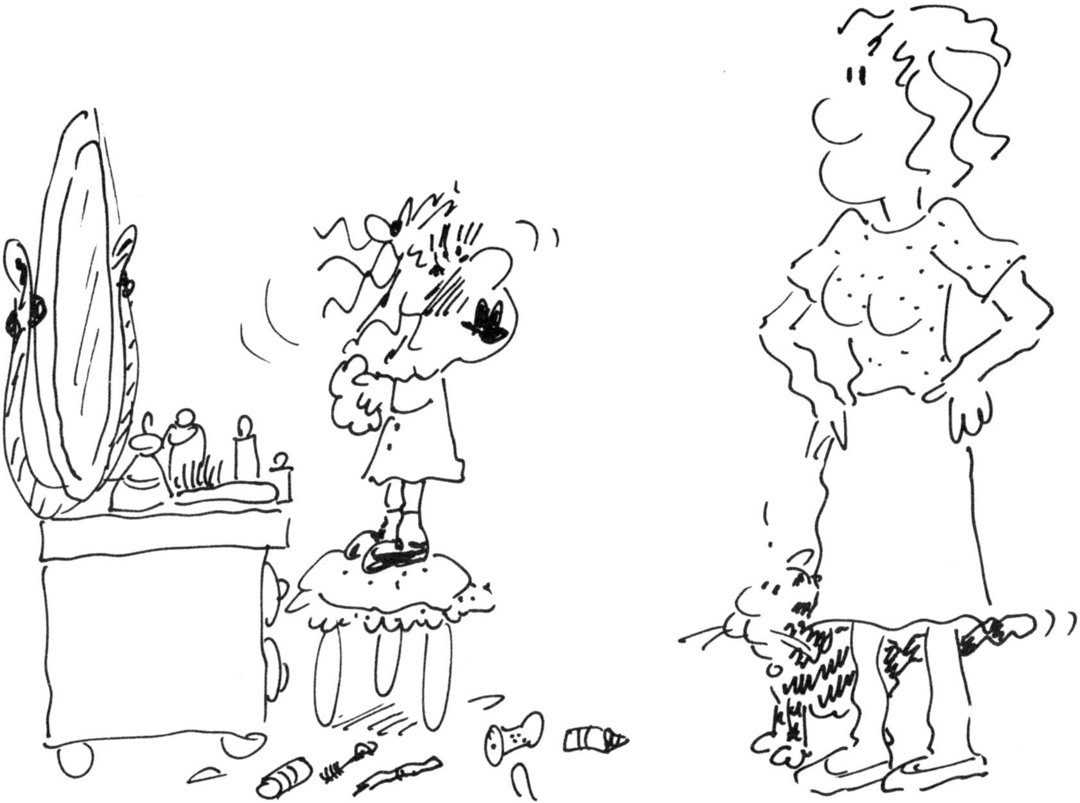

Cats don't eat up all the
food in the fridge.

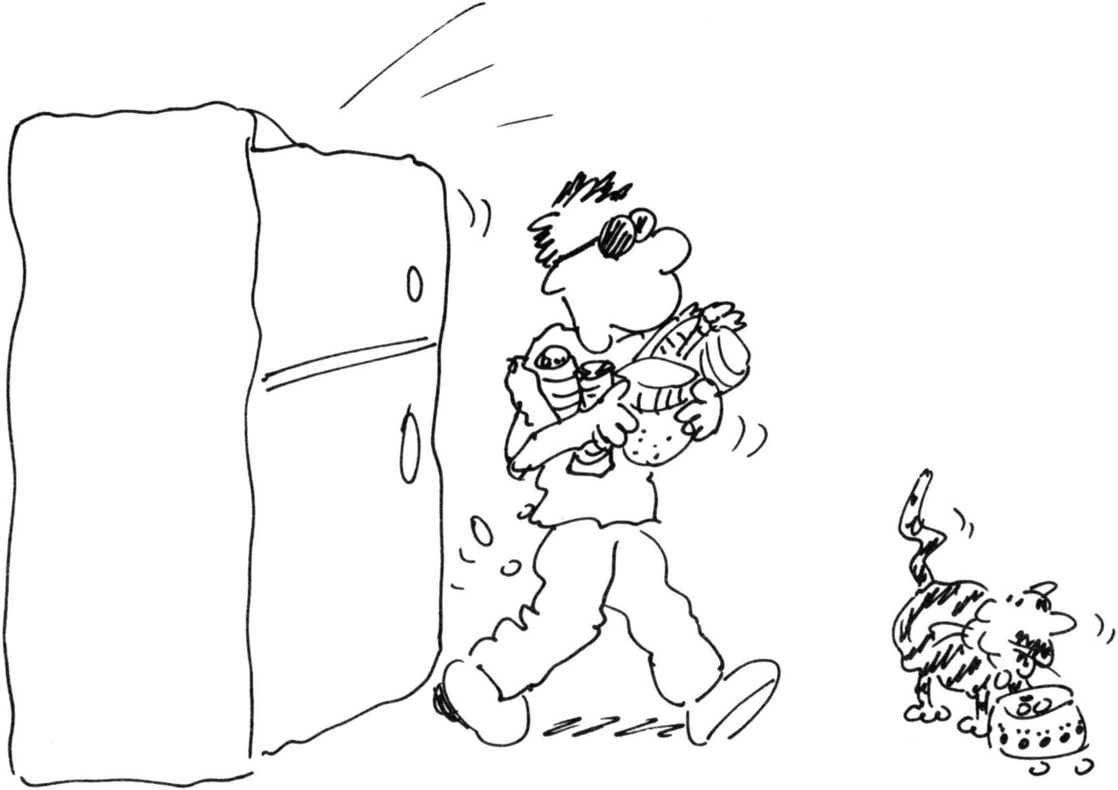

A cat would never wait till
bed time to tell you to bake
something for the next day.

you're supposed to bake little cakes for my class party tomorrow morning.
Z Z
Z Z

Cats never try to make
you feel guilty or bad.

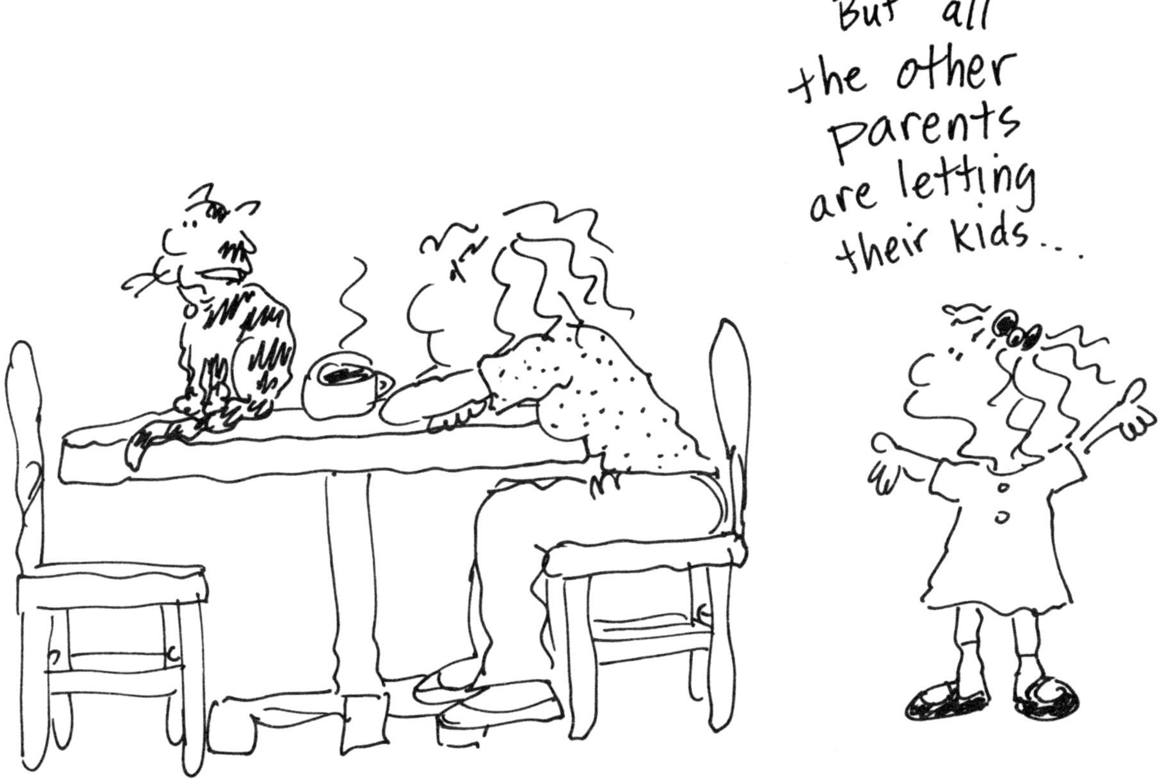
But all the other parents are letting their kids...

Cats never want to get anything pierced.

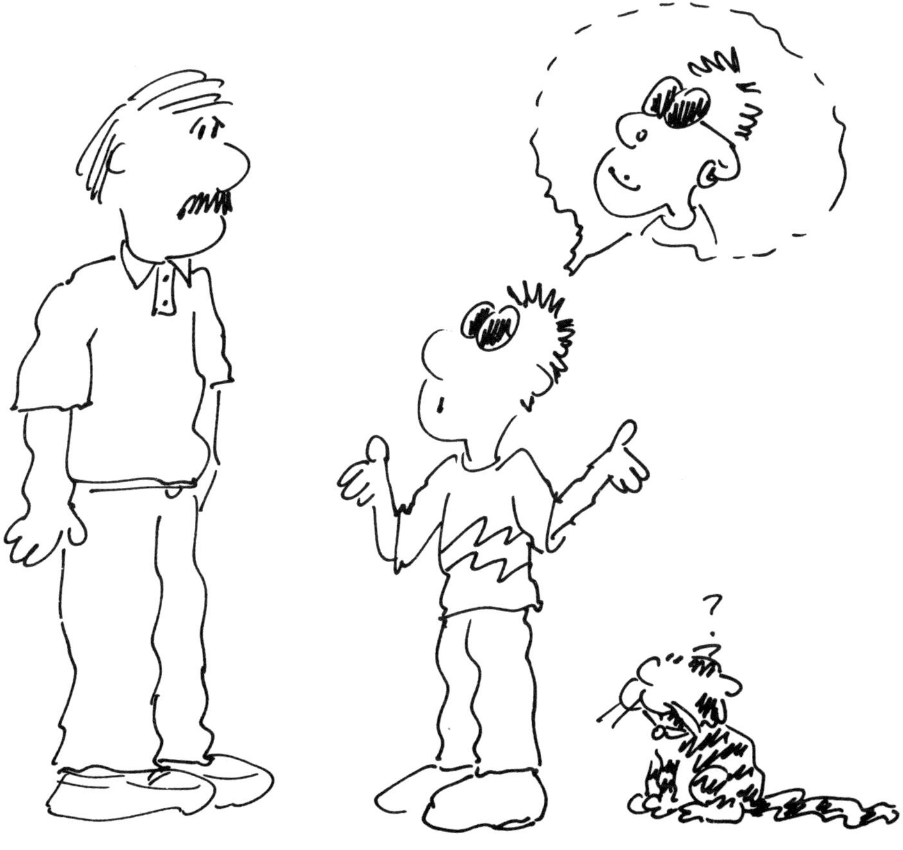

Cats don't bring home
little friends.

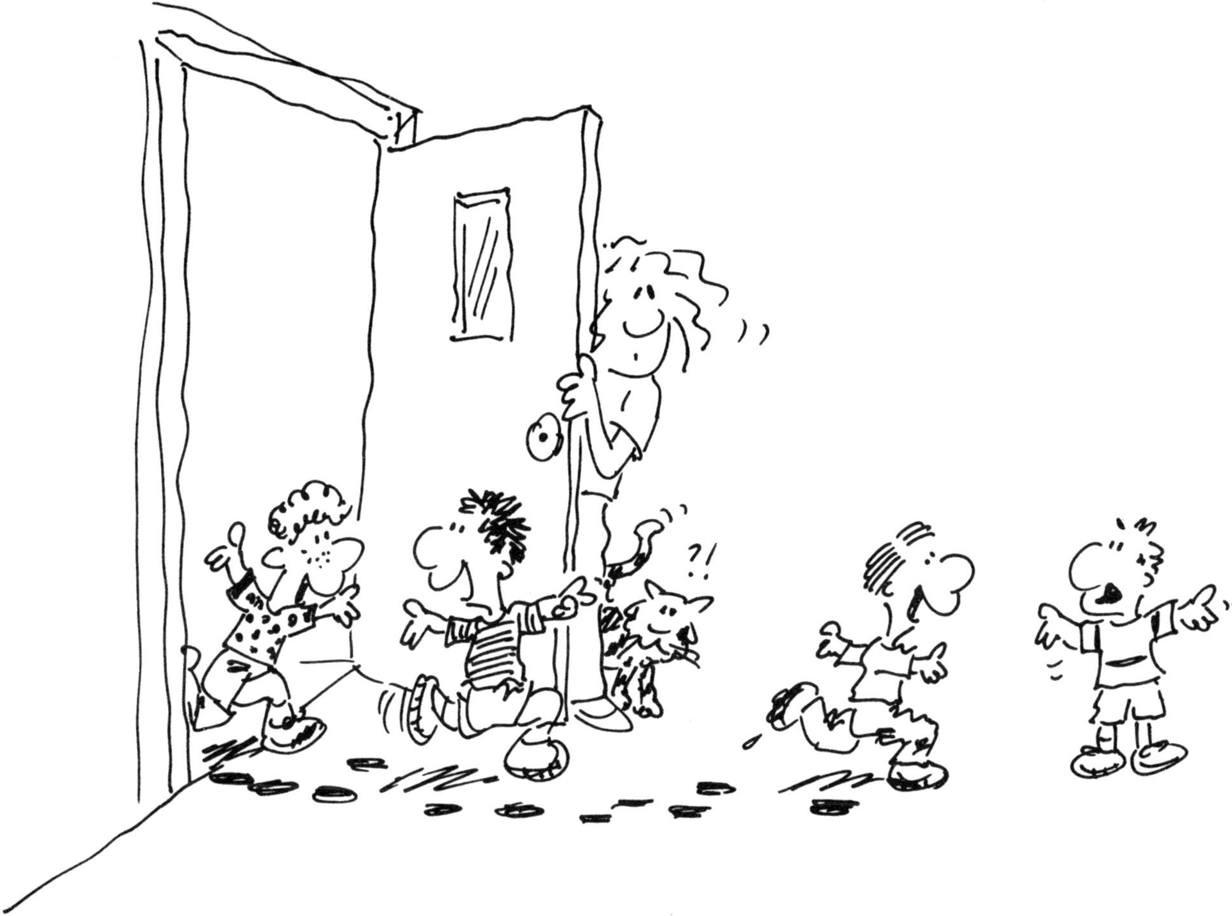
?!

Cats never embarrass
you in public.

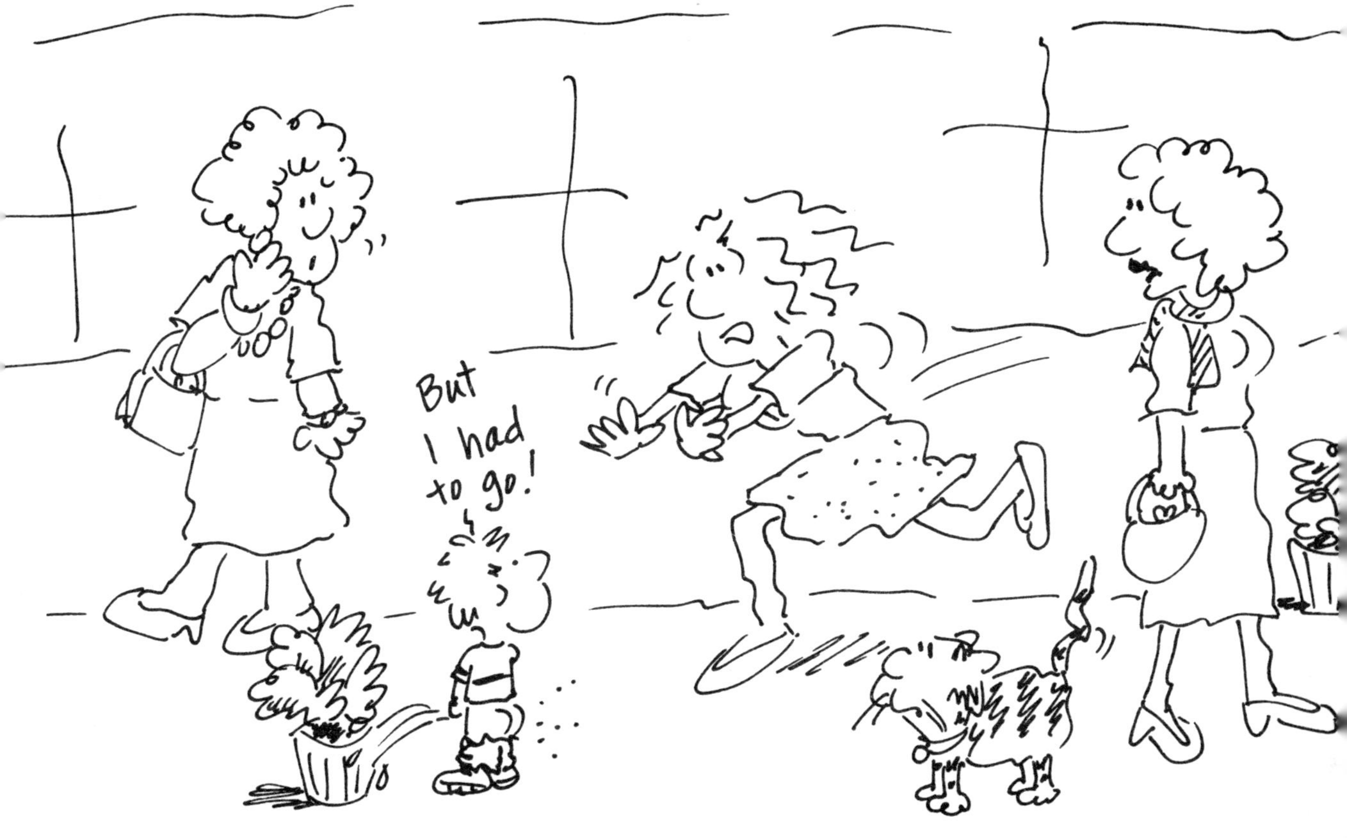
But I had to go!

You don't have to give a
cat pocket money.

You never get calls from
your cat's teacher.

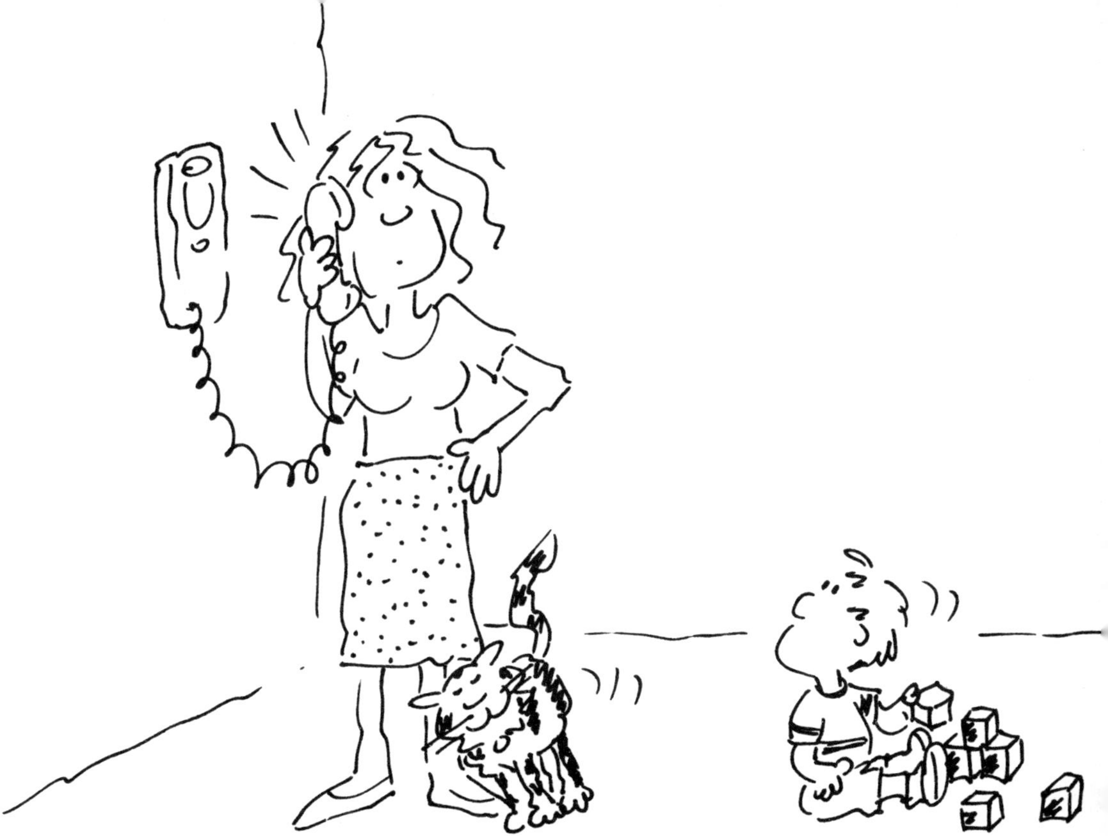

You never have to argue with
a cat about the way it
wears its hair.

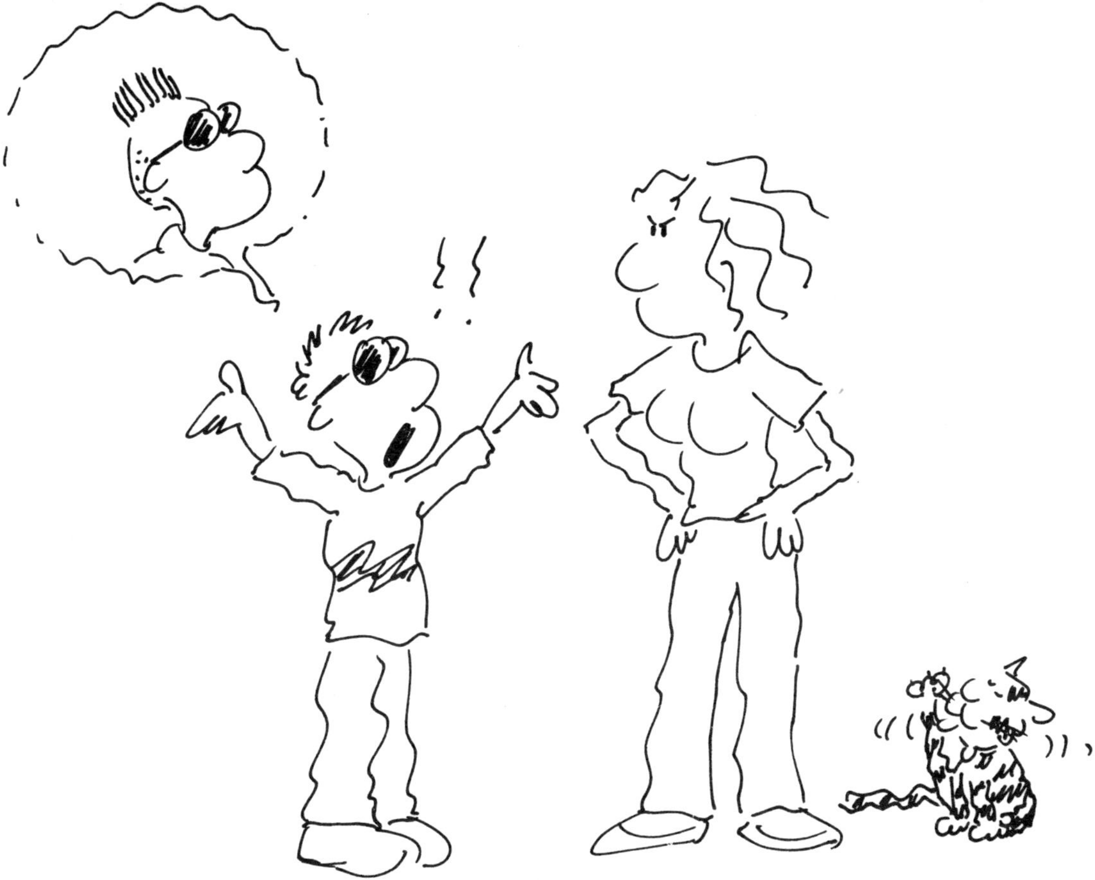

You never have to make
a cat a costume for
a school play.

You never have to help a
cat with homework.

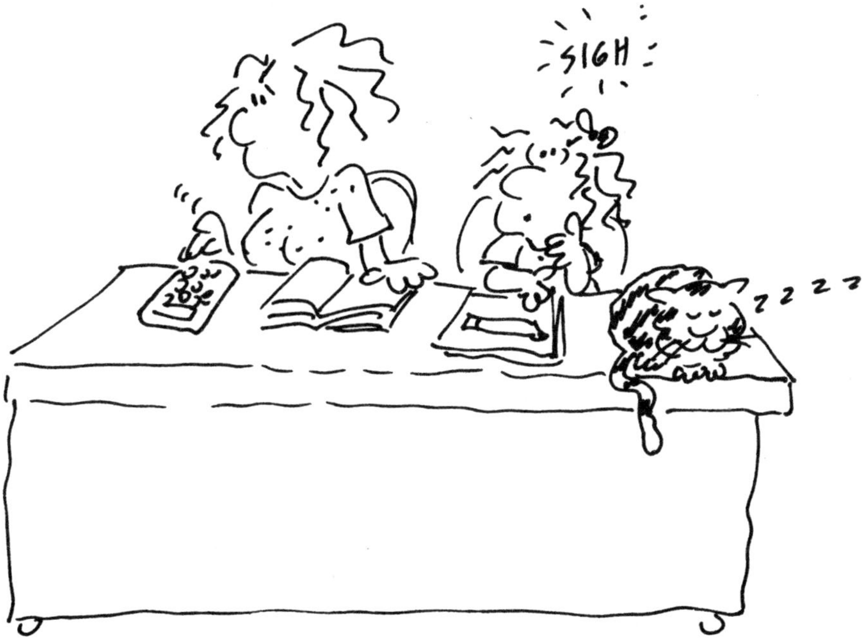
SIGH
z z z z z

You don't have to dress
a cat.

Cats don't need braces.

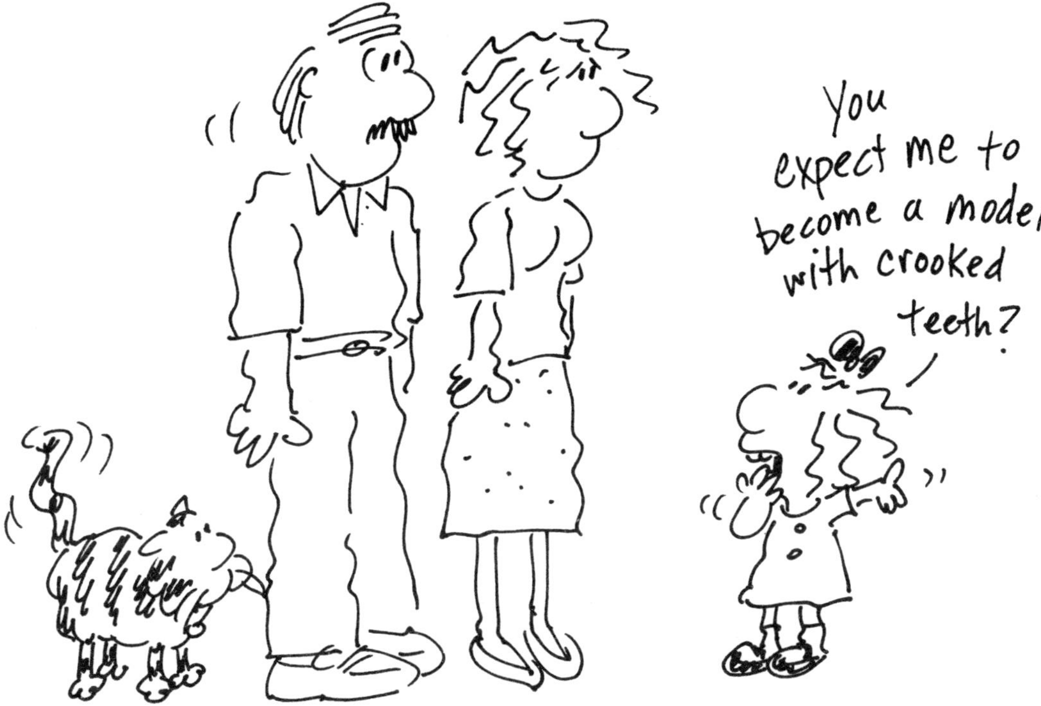
You expect me to become a model with crooked teeth?

You don't have to teach
a cat manners.

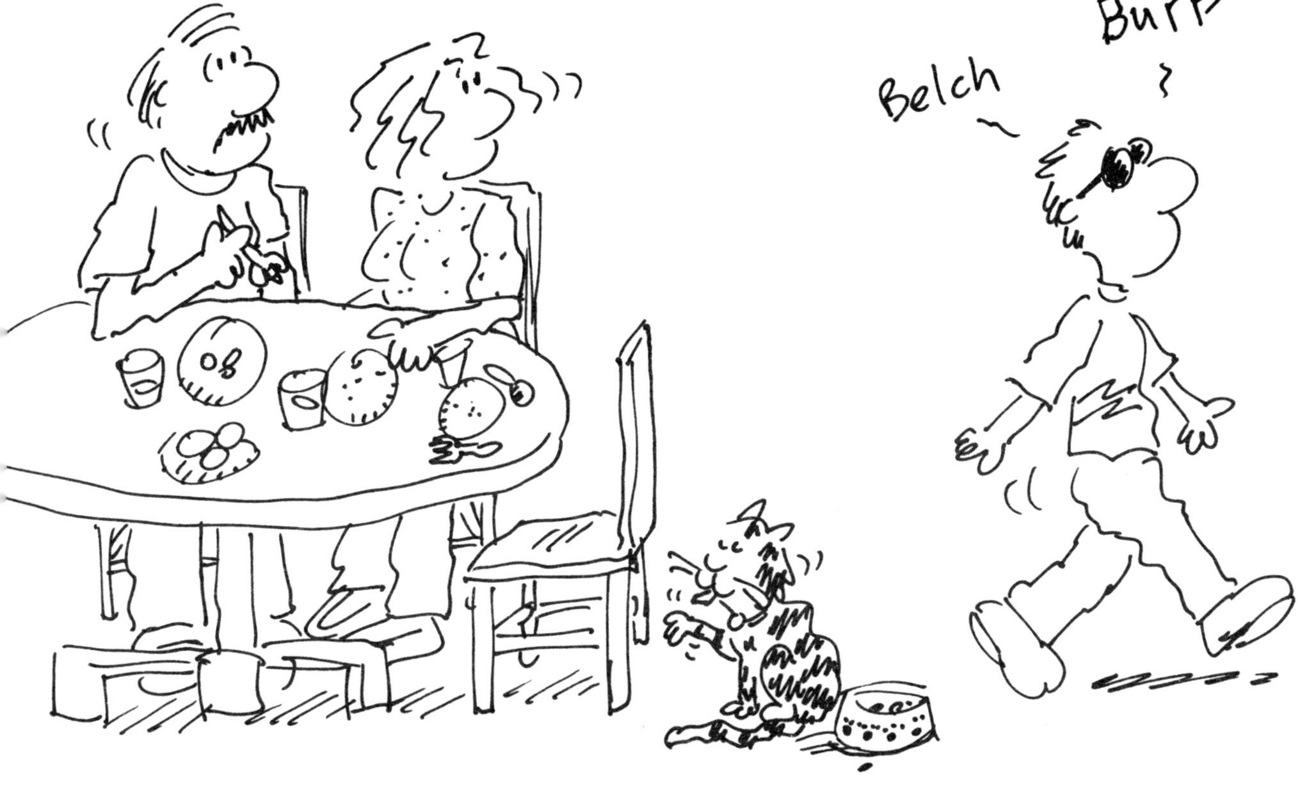
Belch
Burp

You can get a cat fixed.

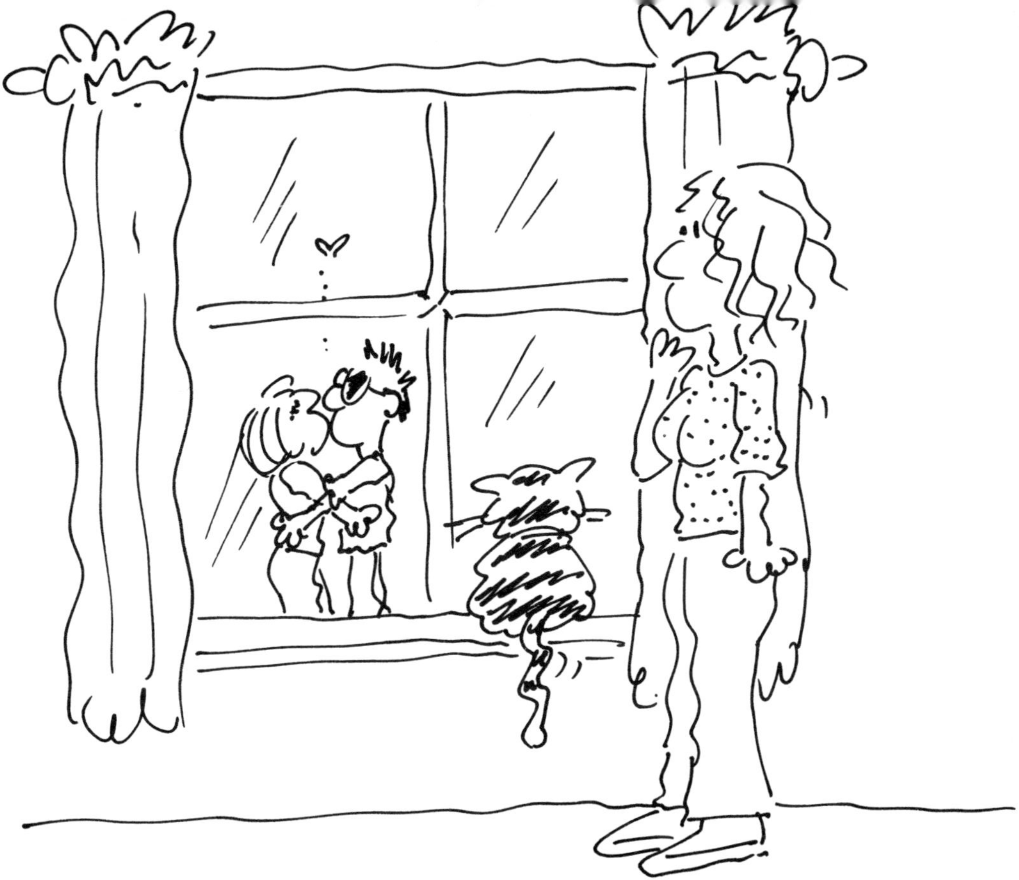

Cats don't have parties
when you're away.

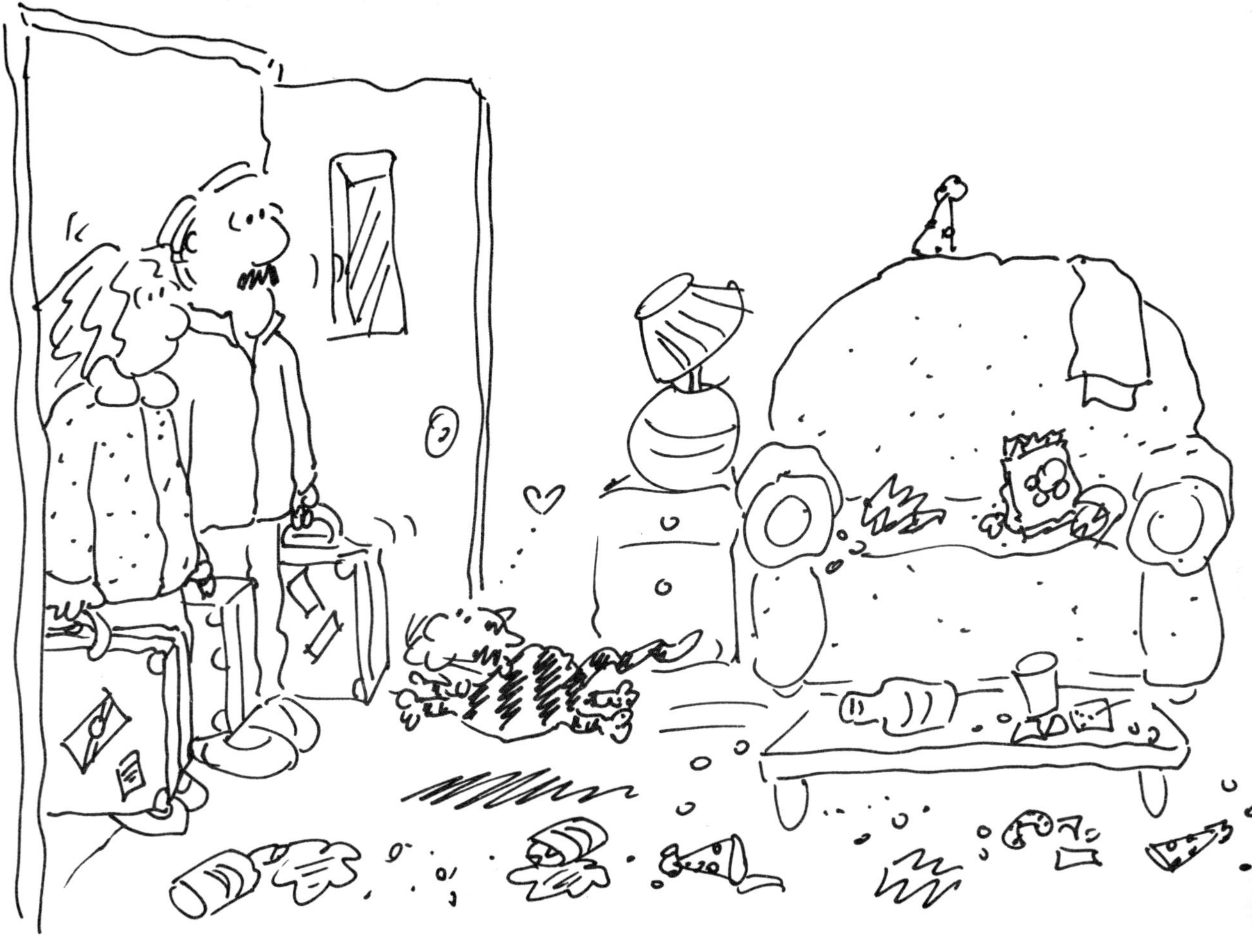

You never worry if a cat will
ever grow up and amount
to anything in life.

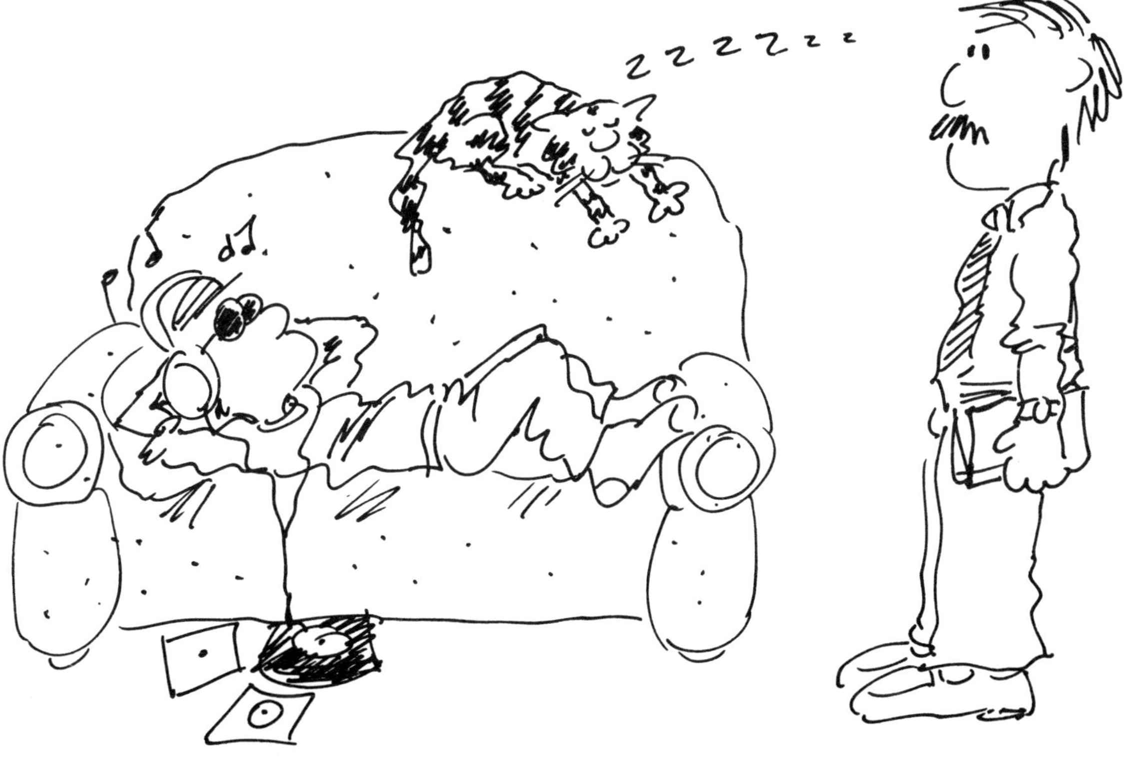
zzzzzzzz

You don't have to send a
cat to school or college.

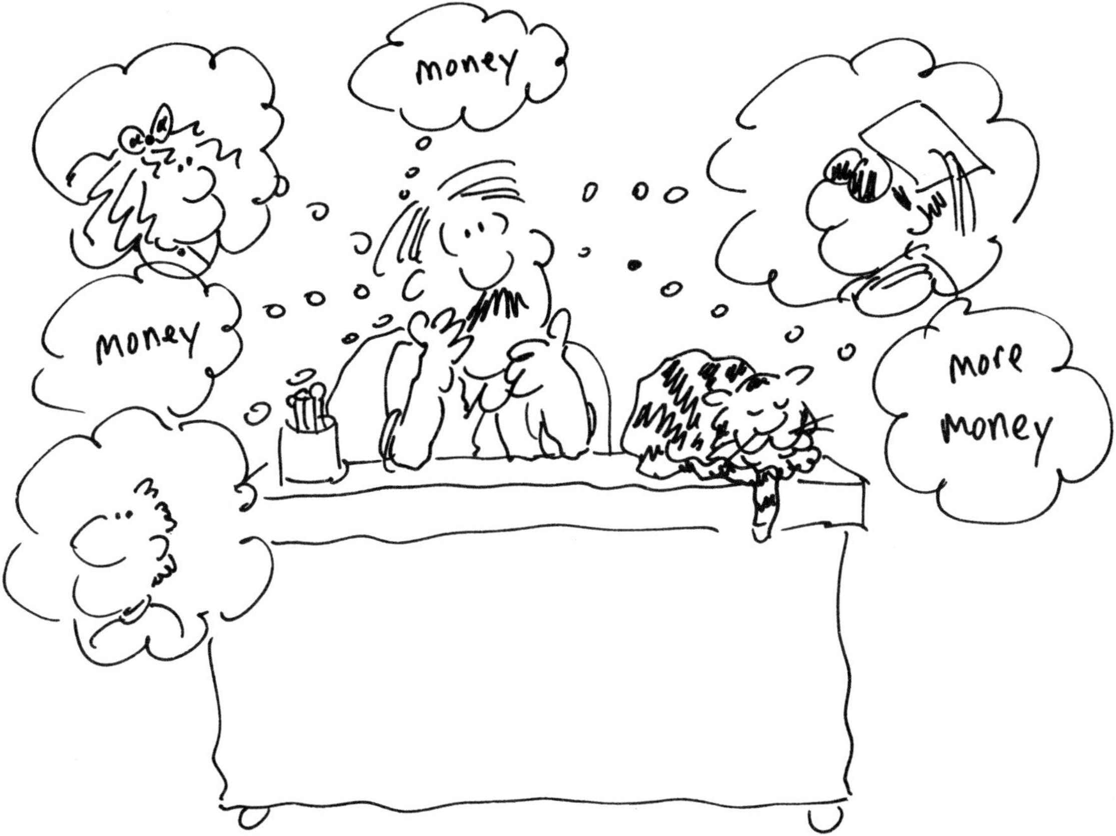
money
money
more money

A cat would never try
to blackmail you.

If you let me go to Andy's party, I won't tell Dad how much money you spent on that new dress.

AND...

Cats always make you
feel loved.

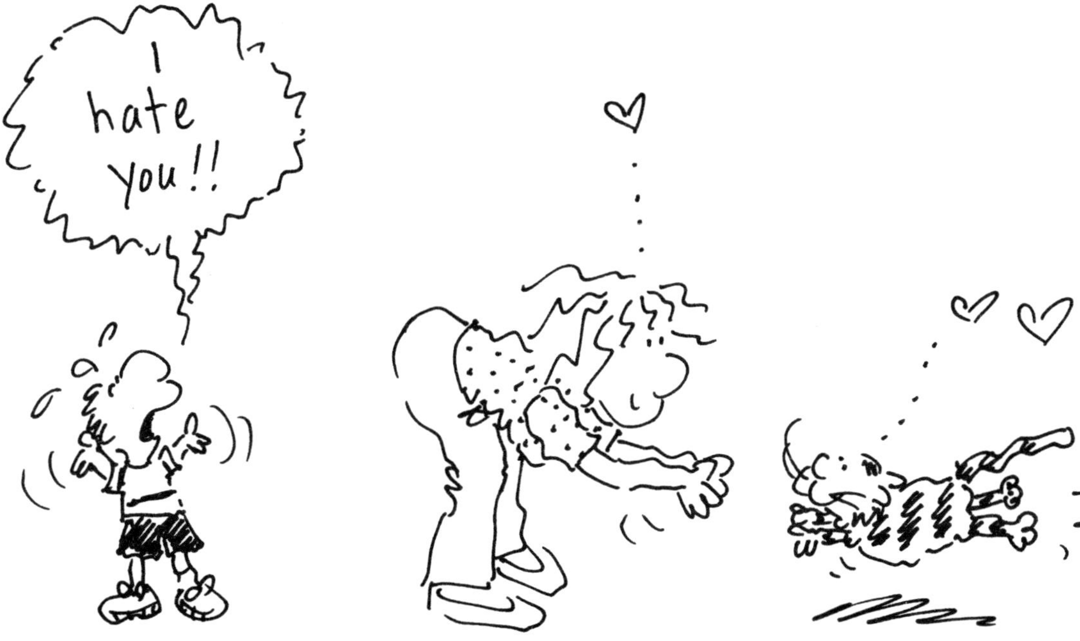
I hate you!!